chunky crochet

Amanda Ljunggren

chunky crochet

16 garments, accessories and homewares to get hooked on

INTRODUCTION

PROJECTS

It all started with a potholder

I first picked up a crochet hook in spring 2020. The short version of the story is that it felt like a whole new world of textiles opened up before my eyes – a world filled with colour, shape, texture and unlimited opportunities. A ball of wool could become practically anything I could think of.

The long version of the story is that I battled with my potholder for days on end before it was finished and the end result was such a wonky, ugly little square – not that it was actually square – that I decided to make a new one IMMEDIATELY. This meant I kept on working away at the same pattern over and over again until finally I'd made a potholder with reasonably straight edges and even stitches.

Soon enough, it was as if crochet had cast a spell on me. I always had a new project on my hook. It wasn't long before I'd stopped following other people's crochet patterns and started designing my own.

In October 2021, I launched my collection of crocheted clothing in Vogue, and I haven't put my hook down since.

Textiles are a broad art form, in the sense that your textile creations can take different practical and aesthetic forms. If the textile is on the floor, it's a rug. If it's hanging on the wall, it's art. If we wear it, it's clothing. If it's on the kitchen table, it's a table cloth. On the sofa, it's a throw, and if it's hanging up in the window, it's a curtain. The possibilities are endless and that's what makes textiles such fun to play around with.

Use the patterns in this book as a guide rather than as instructions set in stone telling you exactly how you should create your crochet projects. Feel free to lengthen, shorten or extend them however you fancy. Or maybe launch straight into designing your own patterns using mine as a guide. There are no rules. When our creativity takes off, we open ourselves up to something magical. If the urge strikes, grab it and enjoy it!

Whoever you are and for whatever reason you happen to be holding this book, I hope it inspires you to crochet something big of your own.

Amanda Ljunggren

7.0mm
8.0mm
9.0mm
12.00mm

Crochet hooks & yarn

CHOOSING YOUR CROCHET HOOK

There are many different kinds of crochet hooks so it's worth trying out a few different ones to see which you prefer. However, it can be difficult to work out which type of crochet hook you like best before you've learned the basics or worked your way through your first crochet project.

My favourite hooks are made from aluminium – they are lightweight and allow me to crochet for hours without my hands getting tired. They also have good friction – the yarn slides easily over the hook making my crochet flow smoothly.

Crochet hooks come in two different shapes: inline and tapered. An inline hook has a pointed top and the curved end of the hook is the same width as the shaft. It has a sharp, straight tip on the inside of the hook. A tapered crochet hook has a softer hook, which gets narrower towards the curve of the hook. Personally, I prefer a tapered hook. I started crocheting with an inline hook and found it awkward and clunky to use, but when I switched to a tapered hook, it just clicked. The yarn was easier to pull through and my stitches were straighter. But even the curve of your crochet hook is often a matter of personal taste.

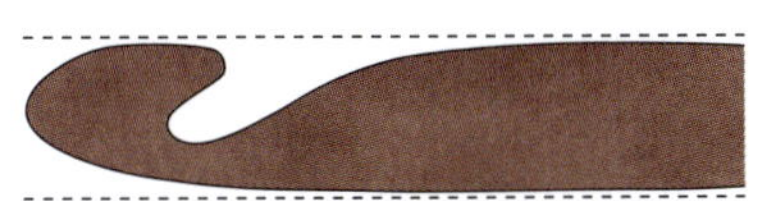

Inline

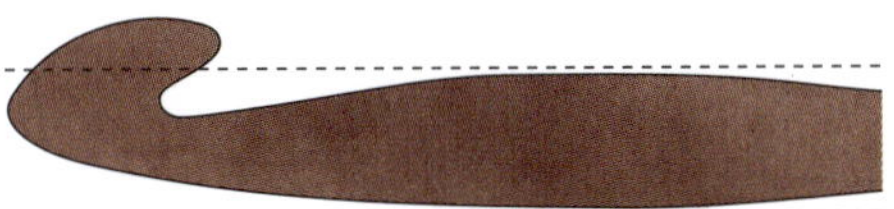

Tapered

Choose the size of your crochet hook based on the thickness of the yarn you will be using. The thicker the yarn, the bigger the hook you will need and vice versa.

Hook sizes may be given in millimetres or you might find crochet hooks that use letters or different numbers to denote sizes, from the UK or US. The patterns in this book use 7 mm, 8 mm, 9 mm and 12 mm crochet hooks (US K/10½ and above, L/11, N/13 and P/16 or above).

It's useful to buy a whole set of crochet hooks. They are often sold together in sizes of 2–10 mm, which will work for the vast majority of patterns, not just the ones in this book. You may need to buy bigger hooks (over 10 mm) separately. You can often find crochet hooks in your local craft shop.

YARN

The most important thing when choosing yarn is to choose something you like looking at and working with. Go for something that feels inspiring – like a yarn that's heavenly soft or something with beautiful colours. The more you love your materials, the more you're going to enjoy the process. If you start crocheting with your yarn and can't stand working with it, it's unlikely you're going to be happy with the process, or with the end result either.

Personally, I prefer using natural materials in all my projects. Yarns from natural fibres are a bit more expensive than synthetic yarn but I'd still recommend them; your projects will age better and be easier to care for.

Natural materials breathe, which means the clothes you make from them are more comfortable. Wool and cotton also have self-cleaning properties, so you can clean your clothes just by hanging them up outside to air.

Natural fibres have a strength and texture that I really love. The yarns I use in the book are:

MERINO WOOL & BRITISH NATURAL WOOL

Wool yarns are renowned for their amazing quality and their self-cleaning ability. They keep you warm, are compostable, and the material shapes itself to your body. In other words, this means the more you wear your wool sweaters, the better they will fit you.

Merino wool is incredibly soft. It slides beautifully between your fingers so you can enjoy your crochet project every step of the way. British natural wool is untreated – from the sheep to your crochet hook – with all the wonderful characteristics untreated wool has to offer.

JUTE

Unlike merino wool, jute isn't as soft or as comfortable for your hands to work with. This means it's used for completely different reasons; it's firm and hard, so it provides great structure for practical projects that must withstand everything life can throw at them, such as bags or interior design projects. Jute is also compostable.

COTTON

Cotton yarn is a material with many uses because, just like wool, it has self-cleaning properties and is compostable. But unlike wool, cotton is cool, making it perfect to use for spring and summer wear.

COTTON RIBBON YARN

Ribbon is a cable-spun, flat cotton yarn without stretch, which works brilliantly for projects that need to keep their shape well, such as bags and accessories.

Ribbon is often confused with t-shirt yarn, despite them having quite different properties and therefore behaving very differently in your crochet projects. T-shirt yarn is also a flat yarn with rolled edges but it is very stretchy.

COTTON YARN FOR MACRAMÉ

The thickest yarn in the book, a perfect choice for projects where you want a robust, resilient structure. You can create sturdy projects using this yarn and a crochet hook at least 12 mm (US P/16) in size.

Macramé yarn is soft and gentle which means you can use it for clothing worn close to the skin. It might not be the best choice for a fitted garment, but it's definitely a good choice for a vest or jacket to sling over your shoulders on a cool summer evening, and it's also a great yarn for home-made interior design projects.

YARDAGE & AMOUNTS USED

Each project states the type of yarn and how much you need. Yardage – the amount of yarn yards or metres per 100 g (3½ oz) or per ball – can vary a lot depending on the type of yarn. For example, a ball of thin yarn will have longer yardage than a thick yarn.

It's worth buying more yarn than the amount stated for the project – that way, you don't have to worry about running out of yarn before you've finished, and if you have yarn left over, you can always use it in your next project.

If you want to use a different yarn from the one stated in the pattern, this will usually work if it's the same type and the same weight. If you want to use a completely different type of yarn or use several thinner yarns together to achieve the same thickness, feel free to experiment. But bear in mind that the drape and texture of your project may turn out differently from the project in the book and that the yarn amounts stated will no longer apply.

The yarn amounts shown are a guideline and may vary depending on how tightly or loosely you crochet. If you want more information about the yarns used in this book, you'll find all the details on page 136.

TENSION (GAUGE)

A tension swatch is a crocheted test square that you make before starting a pattern to see whether you crochet to the same tension (crochet as tightly or as loosely) as stated in the pattern.

The easiest way is to crochet a square 15 x 15 cm (6 x 6 in) and measure how many stitches you have in an area measuring 10 x 10 cm (4 x 4 in). You can then compare that with the tension stated at the start of the pattern.

Depending on how tightly or loosely you crochet compared to the tension for the pattern, you can change your tension at this point by swapping to a bigger or smaller crochet hook, or just use the same hook and crochet more tightly or more loosely. But don't let the idea of having to work a swatch put you off starting to crochet straight away. You can learn more about swatches and tension later.

My personal approach to swatches is fairly laid back. I tend to work on the basis of a process of elimination: Does the type of project need to be a specific size? If the answer is no (which it often is if I'm about to crochet a bag, a scarf or an interior decor project), I don't usually worry about checking my tension because it doesn't really matter if my bag comes out a bit bigger or smaller than the measurements in the pattern.

On the other hand, if you're making clothes and they need to actually fit (like a pair of trousers or any other kinds of garment where the pattern is designed for a range of sizes), it's best to work a swatch to make sure your final project comes out the size you want and fits you. If you like your crocheted clothes oversized, the easy option is to go up one or two sizes and so avoid having to do a swatch anyway – because even if you're crocheting too tightly, the garment will probably still fit because you went up a size to begin with.

Personally, I'm not that fussy about double-checking my tension before I launch into a pattern, but if you choose to do it my way, you need to be aware that there's a risk your crocheted shorts might end up more like a pair of hot pants.

0087
FIBER-GLASS

OTHER EQUIPMENT

Besides yarn and crochet hooks, there are a few other things it's handy to have:

SCISSORS

Any scissors will do, whatever you've got hanging around in the kitchen or in a drawer.

DARNING NEEDLES

It's worth having a few darning needles in different sizes to sew in the loose ends of your finished crochet projects.

STITCH MARKERS

Stitch markers are used to mark stitches during work in progress. They often look a bit like a paperclip. There are lots of different kinds of stitch markers but ordinary safety pins or hairpins often work just as well.

PENCIL & ERASER

An easy way to mark where you are in the pattern and make personal notes as you go along.

COUNTER

A non–essential but quite helpful piece of equipment that you can use to count your rows, rounds or stitches. It's especially handy if you tend to put your project down mid-way, wander off and come back to it later.

TAPE MEASURE

Always useful to have around, especially if you are making garments with a specific fit, measuring the length of a shoulder strap for a bag, or making up a sweater.

SEWING THREAD

I use ordinary cotton sewing thread to sew the different parts of a project together, like when joining granny squares to make a blanket. I prefer using thread with a shiny surface. This helps the thread to slide smoothly through the yarn when you are sewing sections of crochet together.

Getting started

You can hold your crochet hook and yarn however you want to, as long as it works for you and you are crocheting smoothly and evenly. However, most people tend to hold their crochet hook either in a pencil or a knife grip. Try holding your hook both ways and see which works best for you. One often feels more natural than the other.

I prefer placing the yarn round my little finger and letting it run free across my hand. Lots of crocheters want more control over their yarn than that and wind it around a couple of fingers or make a loop around their little finger. It's worth trying a couple of different ways of holding your yarn before starting on your first project.

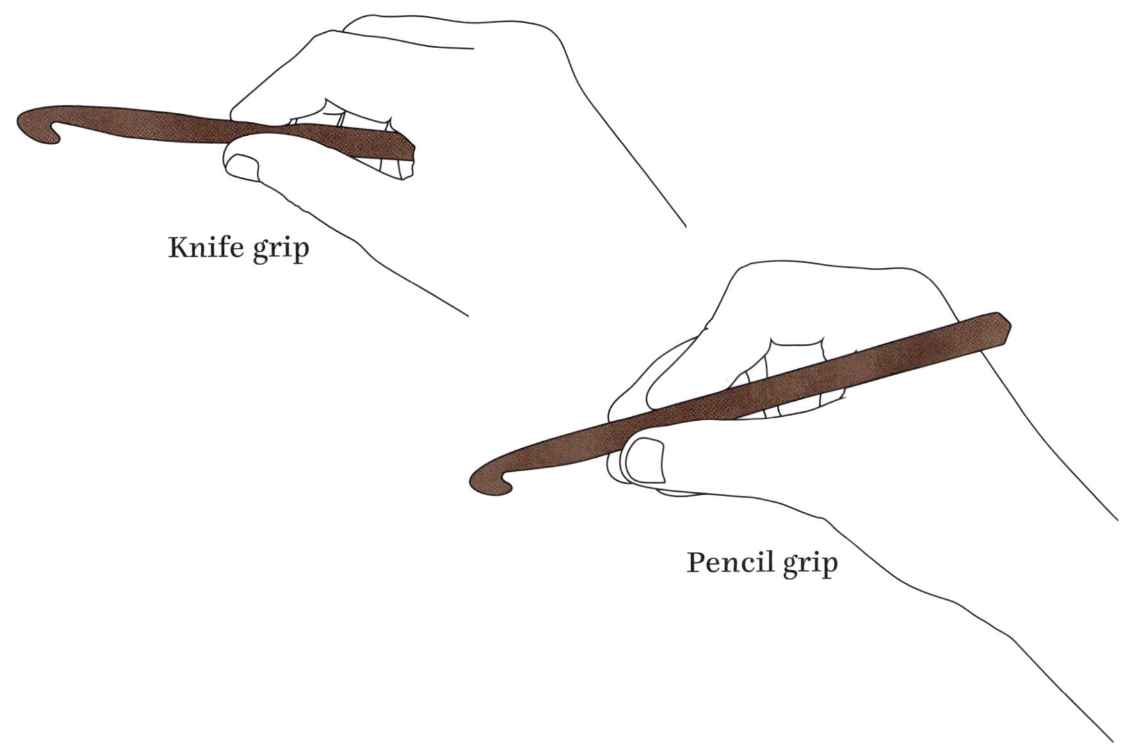

BASIC CROCHET STITCHES

Crochet is made up of several basic stitches that you will need to learn; these are illustrated below. This book uses UK crochet terms but I've added the US terms here for your reference. To start working the basic stitches, you first need to make a slip knot.

SLIP KNOT

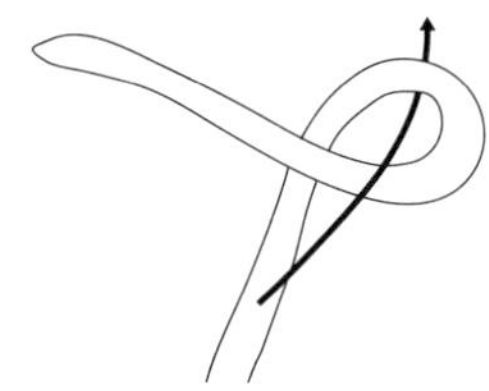

1. Place the tail of the yarn over the yarn coming from the ball to make a loop.

2. Pull the yarn coming from the ball through the loop.

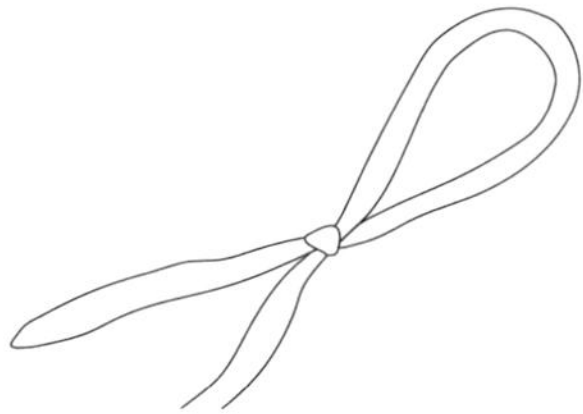

3. Pull gently on the tail of the yarn.

4. Place the slip knot on your hook and pull on the yarn ball end to adjust the size.

CHAIN STITCH (CH)

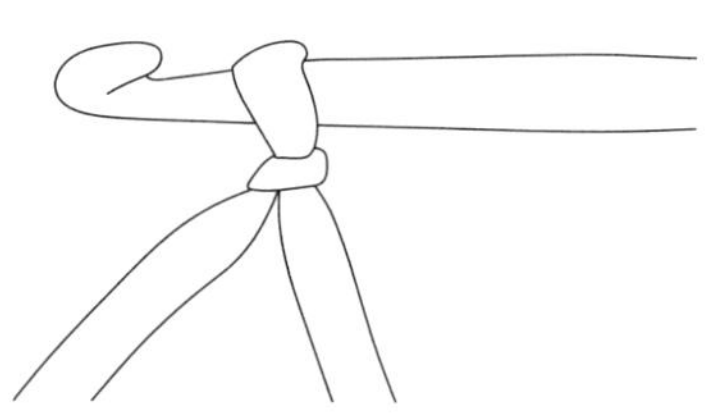

1. Start with a slip knot on your hook.

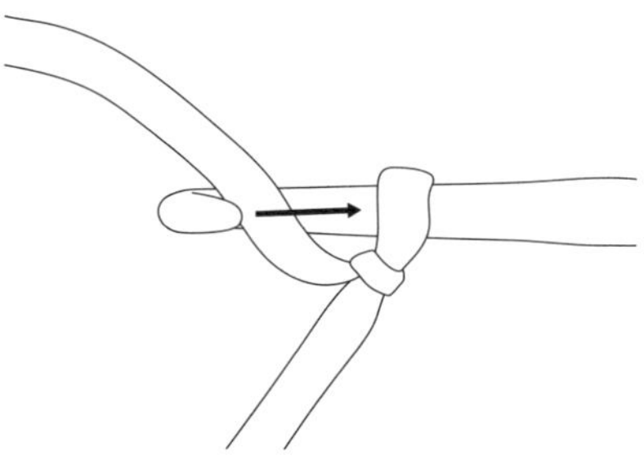

2. Wrap the yarn over the hook and pull it through the loop on your hook.

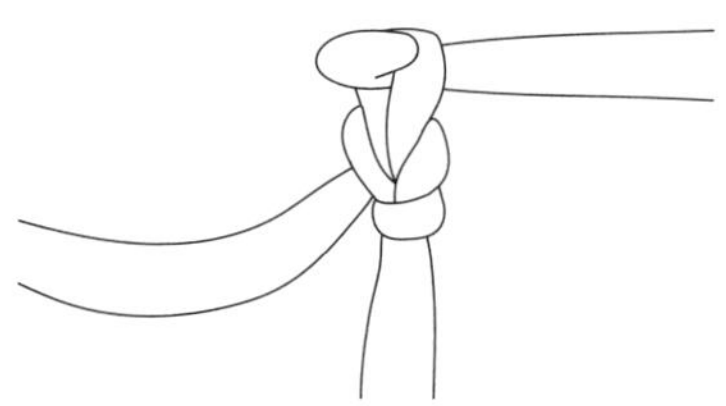

3. Completed chain stitch.

4. Repeat until you have the number of chain stitches you need (this is called a chain).

SLIP STITCH (SL ST)

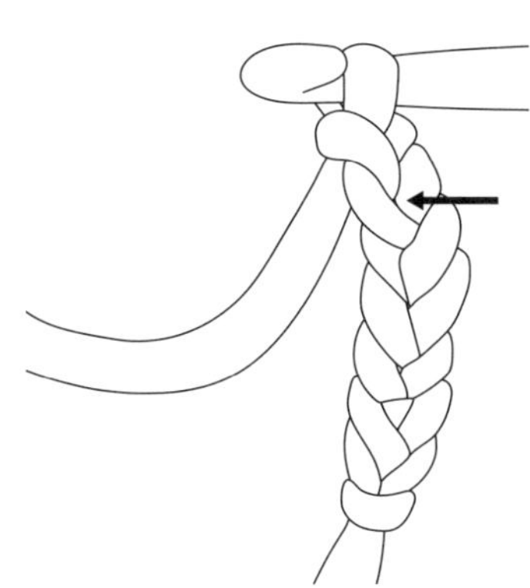

1. Insert your hook into a stitch in your work.

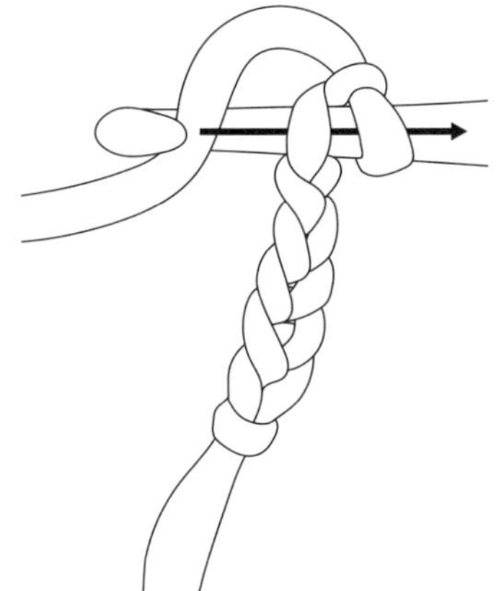

2. Wrap the yarn over the hook and pull it through both loops on the hook.

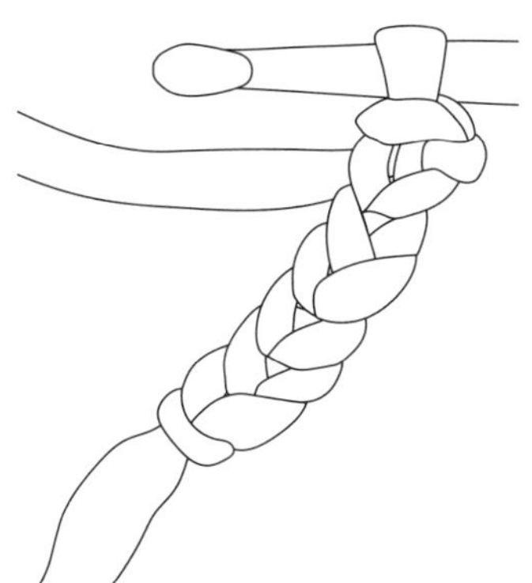

3. Completed slip stitch.

DOUBLE CROCHET (DC) / US SINGLE CROCHET

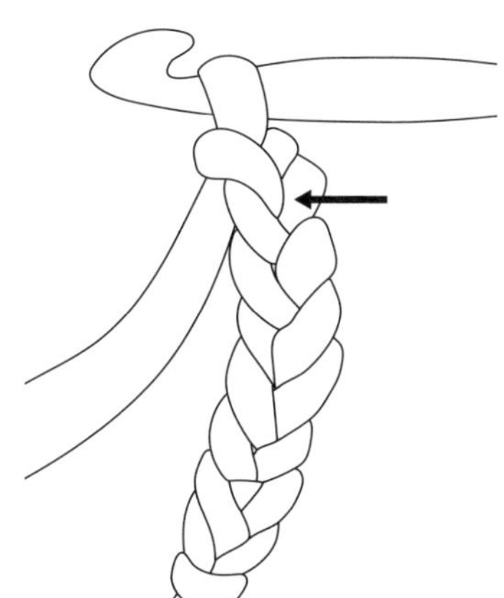

1. Insert your hook into the second chain from the hook/a stitch in your work. Wrap the yarn over the hook and pull it through the stitch.

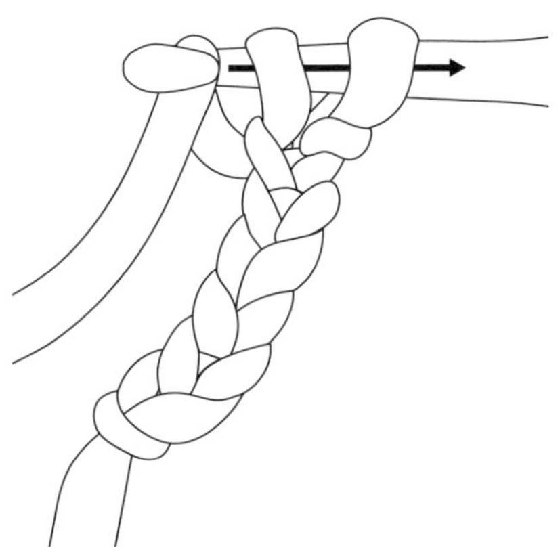

2. You now have two loops on your hook. Wrap the yarn over the hook again and pull it through both loops.

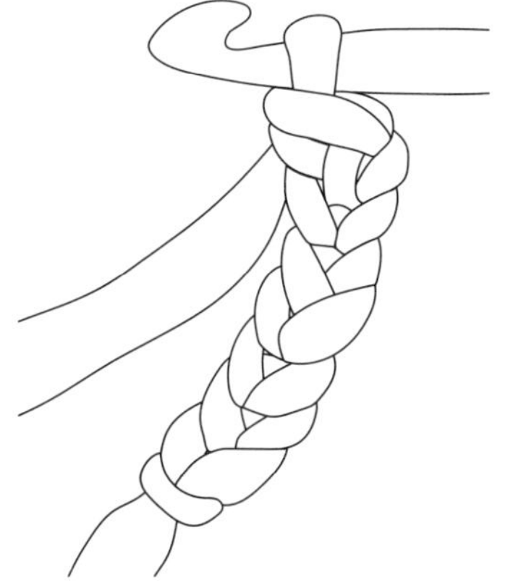

3. Completed double crochet.

TREBLE CROCHET (TR) / US DOUBLE CROCHET

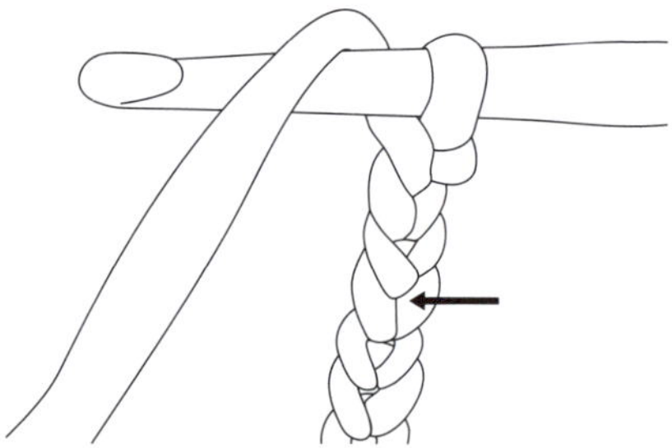

1. Wrap the yarn over your hook and then insert the hook into the fourth chain from the hook/ a stitch in your work.

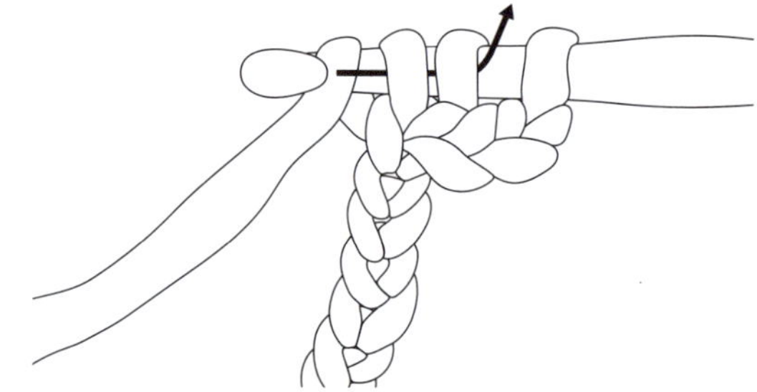

2. Wrap the yarn over the hook again and pull it through the stitch. You now have three loops on your hook. Wrap the yarn around the hook again and pull it through the first two loops.

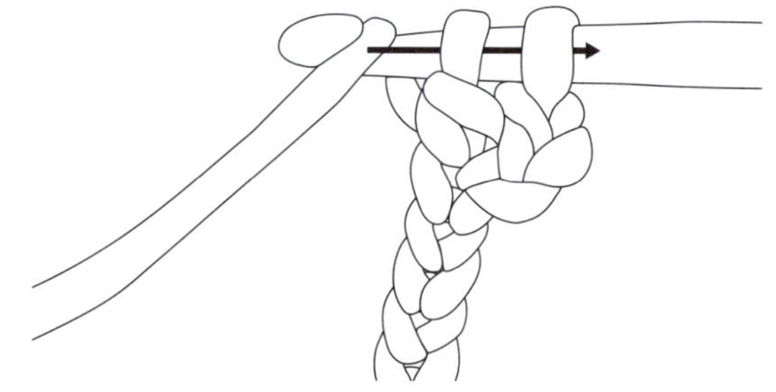

3. Wrap the yarn around the hook a third time and pull it through the remaining two loops.

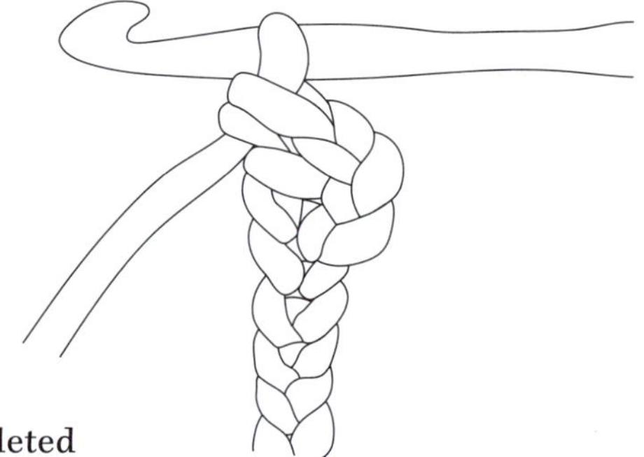

4. Completed treble crochet.

FRONT AND BACK LOOPS

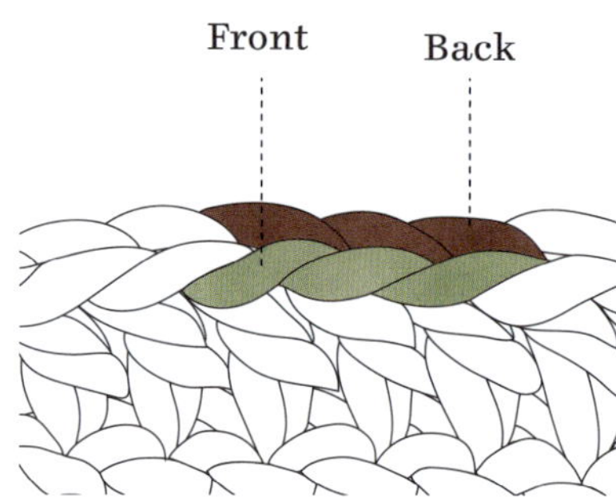

You will usually work into both the front and back loops of a stitch but in a couple of patterns, you will need to only insert your hook into the front loop (front loop only = FLO) or back loop (back loop only = BLO) of the stitch.

CHANGING COLOUR

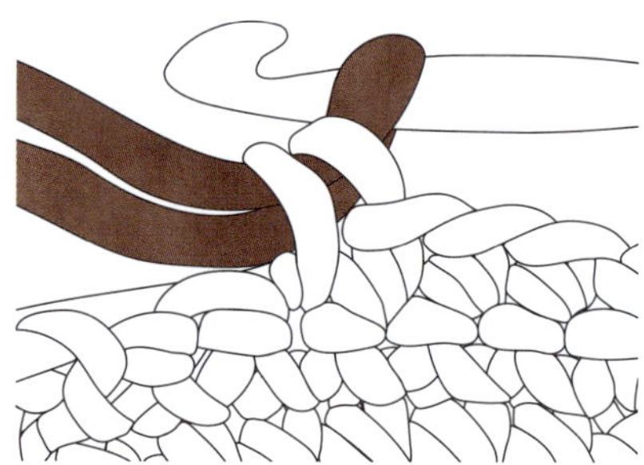

If you want to change colour, finish the last step of your stitch with the new colour as it makes the colour change look neater.

FASTENING OFF

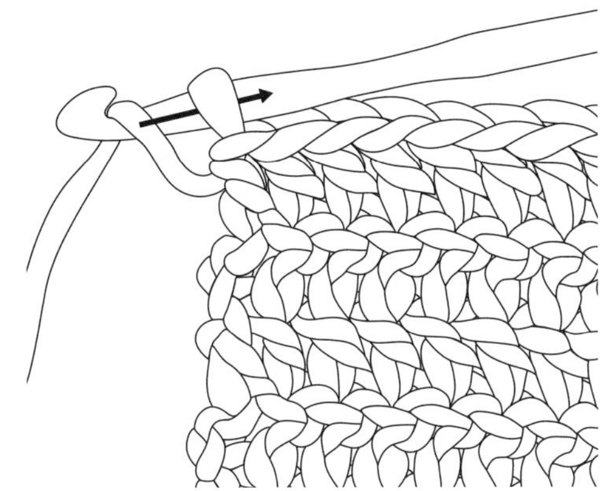

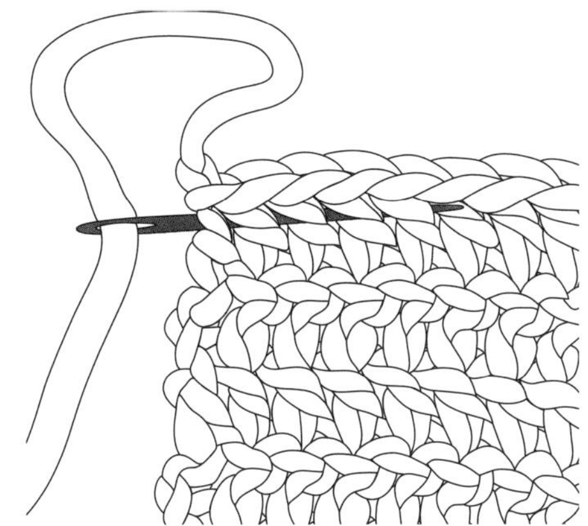

Fasten off and secure your work by cutting the yarn and pulling it through the last stitch. Then sew in the loose ends neatly.

OVERCAST STITCH

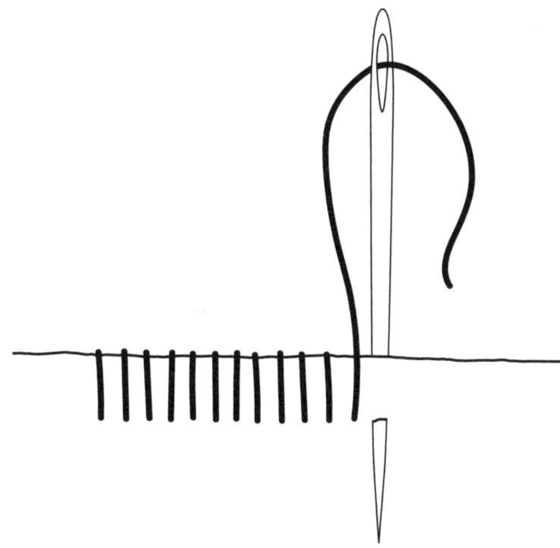

Overcast stitch, also known as whip stitch, is good for sewing different crochet sections together but also for pulling a section together and making it smaller.

MATTRESS STITCH

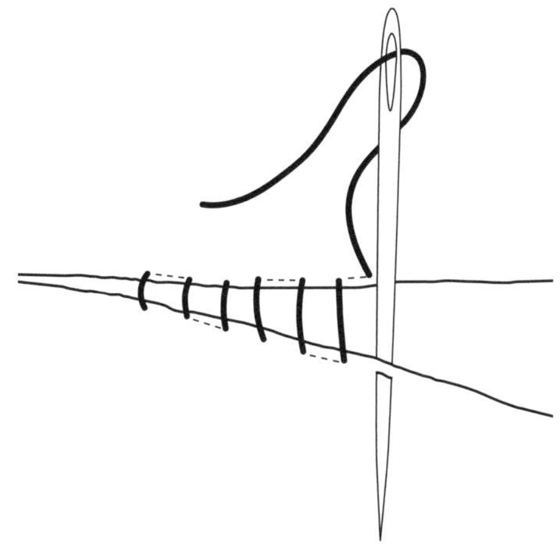

Mattress stitches are made into each crochet stitch and the seam is practically invisible from the right side.

ABBREVIATIONS

ST/STS = stitch/stitches

CH = chain

DC = double crochet (US single crochet)

SL ST = slip stitch

TR = treble crochet (US double crochet)

TOG = together

BLO = back loop only

FLO = front loop only

CH SP = chain space

_ = repeat

READING A CROCHET PATTERN

Getting to grips with a crochet pattern as a beginner isn't always easy. Crochet patterns are written using abbreviations and this can make the crochet learning curve feel quite challenging. But if we break the elements and the abbreviations down, it will make it easier to understand.

Everyone who designs crochet patterns writes in their own unique way – there is no single universal way of writing a pattern. However, there are gudelines and standards that most pattern designers follow. Most patterns start by introducing the project with an information box. This will tell you the name and type of the project, the crochet hook size, the measurements of the finished project, the yarn amount, tension, techniques, materials, etc. There is usually a list of all the abbreviations used in the pattern and what they mean. It's useful to read this information before launching into the pattern itself to get a good overview.

Let's have a look reading the actual pattern and the abbreviations. There are countless different stitches and abbreviations you'll encounter. I've chosen to list only the abbreviations that are relevant to the patterns in this book. All the stitches in the book are explained and illustrated in the section that starts on page 24.

COMMON CROCHET TERMS

SPACE = work into a gap/space between stitches instead of into a stitch.

CHAIN = a chain of chain stitches worked in a row. At the start of the work this is called a foundation chain.

FOUNDATION CHAIN RING = a chain joined with a slip stitch to form a ring at the start of a project that will be worked in the round.

2 DC TOG = decrease 1 stitch by working 2 stitches together in double crochet.
Insert the hook in the first dc, *yarn over hook and pull through* twice (2 loops on hook), insert hook into next dc, yarn over hook and pull through (3 loops on hook), yarn over hook and pull through all loops. (1 stitch decreased)

STITCH MARKER = used to mark one or more stitches to help you to follow the pattern.

TURN = turn the whole work to start working the next row on top of the previous row.

RIGHT SIDE AND WRONG SIDE = indicates the front and back of your crochet. This is most noticeable when working in the round. The right side is the side that is facing you, that will be visible when the project is finished.

BRACKETS & ASTERISKS

_ = indicates that you should repeat the stitches inside the asterisks x times during the current row/round.

( ) or [ ] = can mean different things depending where you are in the pattern:

- It can be used to show that the stitches inside the brackets should be worked together into the same chain space.

  EXAMPLE:
  ROUND 2: *ch 3, *[3 tr, ch 2, 3 tr] in next 2-ch sp* 3 times, [3 tr, ch 2, 2 tr] in next 2-ch sp, end with a sl st into the top of the third chain. (24 tr, 4 x 2-ch sp)*

- A round or row often ends with the total number of stitches in brackets. This is called a stitch count.

  EXAMPLE:
  ROUND 2: *ch 1, 2 dc in every st, sl st into first st. (14 dc)*

- Sometimes brackets are used to mark repeats instead of asterisks. Brackets can also be used to indicate different sizes throughout a pattern i.e. S (M) L (XL).

SLIP KNOT

Whatever pattern you are following, it will always start with a slip knot. This usually isn't stated in the pattern but you can learn how to make one on page 24.

When counting chain stitches, neither the slip knot nor the loop on your hook count as stitches. In other words, 5 ch means 1 slip knot + 5 chain stitches with one loop left on the hook.

TO TURN OR NOT TO TURN

Will your project be worked back and forth or round and round? You will either turn the work and crochet a new row on top of the previous row – back and forth – or crochet in rounds without turning, going round in a spiral.

> **EXAMPLE:**
> **ROW 1:** *ch 13, turn.*
>
> Indicates you will work back and forth.

> **EXAMPLE:**
> *Ch 5 and sl st into first ch to create ring.*
>
> Indicates you will work round and round.

If your project is worked back and forth, you turn the work, and work the first stitch of row 2 into the second chain stitch from your hook.

> **EXAMPLE:**
> **ROW 1:** *ch 13, turn.*
> **ROW 2:** *1 dc in second ch from hook, 11 dc, turn. (12 dc)*

Here, the 13 chain stitches have become 12 dc because the first chain stitch acts as a turning stitch. A turning stitch, or a turning chain, helps to turn the corner and builds the height of the stitches for the next row. The number of turning stitches you need depends on the type of stitch you're using.

Double crochet only needs 1 turning stitch but a taller stitch like treble crochet will need a turning chain of 2 or 3 stitches.

When you are working double crochet, the turning stitches aren't counted in the total stitch count because they disappear into the work; their main purpose is to maintain the shape and height of the work. When you are working treble crochet, the turning chain is often counted as the first treble, but the pattern will usually indicate if this is the case or not.

TIPS FOR BEGINNERS

- Put a bookmark in the page with all the crochet abbreviations so you can flip back to it easily.
- Use light-coloured yarn. It makes it easier to see (and count) your stitches.
- Use stitch markers to mark the start of a round. This makes it easier to see and remember the first stitch, especially when crocheting in the round.
- The first row or round of a pattern is usually the trickiest and most complicated part of a project. Once you are a couple of rows or rounds in, the process gets easier and your crochet gets easier to hold and to work with.
- Don't be a perfectionist! Give yourself the space to make mistakes and learn from them.

SIZING

If you want your crocheted clothes to fit you perfectly, you need to make them the right size for your body. The clothing patterns in this book are designed for four different sizes, S–XL. Find the measurements on page 135. Most of my designs are oversized so if you want a closer fit, I recommend going down a size. In my view, there's only one way to think about sizing: a piece of clothing should be created to fit your body, not the other way round.

To make the patterns as easy to follow as possible, I have written the instructions for each size separately. You just need to choose a size and then follow the description under the heading for that size to the end of the pattern. Elsewhere you will often find different sizes shown in brackets through the whole pattern, e.g. S (M) L (XL) in one set of instructions.

GET CREATIVE

For me, creativity always starts with curiosity. Whether it's about a certain type of material or a finished garment, I use this curiosity to find out more and by following my natural interest, I never run out of inspiration. I pay attention to how the clothes that caught my eye are constructed. I believe we can learn a lot about garment construction by observing the cut, construction and details of clothes that already exist. You'll often find the most unique and inspiring garments in your local vintage or charity shop, so that's a good place to begin. A vintage shop can act as a museum of fashion design where you never know what exhibition you're about to see – and admission is free!

Having a core wardrobe to rely on is a great starting point for designing your own clothes. By that, I don't mean a wardrobe full of posh trousers and black polo-necks, but a personal wardrobe filled with unique clothes that suit you and your personal taste. Go for colours, shapes and garments that speak to you. If you know exactly what colours, cuts and materials you prefer wearing, your wardrobe can act as a foundation for the clothes you design yourself.

What do you wish to achieve with your design? What colours, textures or shapes do you wish to highlight? Choose materials with this in mind. But don't forget to let your yarn influence you too: when it behaves differently from the way you expected, don't cling on to your original idea too much, let go a bit, follow the rhythm of the yarn and let it shape your final creation. Creating something new is all about constantly adapting to the new decisions, problems and opportunities that arise along the way. Learn to embrace the unexpected and accept it as a natural part of the process.

Projects

Potholder

For me, it all started with a pot holder, so naturally that's going to be the first pattern in the book.

A simple pattern in double crochet and chunky cotton yarn, this potholder is the perfect gentle start if you're new to crochet.

CROCHET HOOK: 12 mm (US P/16 or size to achieve tension)
YARN: 24 m/26¼ yd of 4 mm cotton yarn for macramé
EQUIPMENT: darning needle, scissors
STITCHES: chain stitch, slip stitch, double crochet
TENSION (GAUGE): 6.5 sts x 7 rows to 10 x 10 cm (4 x 4 in)
MEASUREMENTS: approx. 20 x 20 cm (7¾ x 7¾ in)
CONSTRUCTION: The potholder is worked in one piece.
TIPS: Don't worry too much about tension. A potholder doesn't need to have exact measurements. But bear in mind that you may need more yarn if you aren't working to the same tension as in the pattern.

METHOD

ROW 1: ch 13, turn.
ROW 2: 1 dc in second ch from hook, 11 dc, turn. (12 dc)
ROW 3: ch 1 (not counted as a stitch here or throughout pattern), 12 dc, turn. (12 dc)
ROWS 4–10: As row 3. (12 dc)
ROW 11: ch 1, 12 dc, ch 8, join your chain of 8 sts with a sl st in the corner to make a little loop. (12 dc, 8 ch)
ROUND 12: *Work a double crochet edge around your potholder:*
ch 1, 11 dc in row ends, ch 1 around the corner, 11 dc, ch 1 around the corner, 11 dc in row ends, ch 1 around the corner, 11 dc, sl st into first dc of round, cut yarn. (44 dc, 4 ch)
Sew in the loose ends with a big darning needle.

Mini bag

A quick crochet project that you'll manage easily even if you're a beginner.

This mini bag is perfect for all those essential items like your phone, wallet and keys.

CROCHET HOOK: 7 mm (US K/10½ and above)
YARN: 1 ball of cotton ribbon yarn, super chunky (super bulky), 125 m/136 yd per 250 g/8¾ oz ball. Amount used: 120 g/4¼ oz
EQUIPMENT: darning needle, scissors
STITCHES: chain stitch, slip stitch, double crochet, treble crochet
TENSION (GAUGE): 11 sts x 12 rows to 10 x 10 cm (4 x 4 in)
SIZE: approx. 13 x 10 x 7 cm (5 x 4 x 2¾ in) excluding the shoulder strap
CONSTRUCTION: The bag is worked in one piece.
TIPS: Don't worry too much about tension. A bag doesn't need to have exact measurements. But bear in mind that you may need more yarn if you aren't working to the same tension as in the pattern.

METHOD

ROW 1: ch 11, turn.
ROW 2: 1 dc in second ch from hook, 9 dc, turn. (10 dc)
ROW 3: ch 1 (not counted as a stitch here or throughout pattern), 10 dc, turn. (10 dc)
ROWS 4–7: As row 3. (10 dc)
ROW 8: ch 1, 10 dc, turn. (10 dc)
Now continue to crochet the mesh by working around the square you just made, working in the round as follows.
ROUND 9: ch 4 (counted as 1 tr + 1 ch here and throughout pattern), skip 1 st, 1 tr in next st, *ch 1, skip 1 st, 1 tr in next st* 16 times, ch 1, sl st into the top of the third chain. (18 tr)
Work a tr in each corner as this will make the shape more stable.
ROUND 10: ch 4, skip 1 st, 1 tr in next st, *ch 1, skip 1 st, 1 tr in next st* 16 times, ch 1, sl st into the top of the third chain. (18 tr)
ROUNDS 11–15: As round 10. (18 tr)
ROUND 16: *Crochet the edge and the straps.*
ch 1, *1 dc in next ch sp, 1 dc in next tr* 7 times, 1 dc in next ch sp, then ch 64 to make the strap on one side, turn, starting in second ch from hook, work 63 dc into the chain, sl st into ch sp at start of ch, ch 1, then *1 dc in next tr, 1 dc in next ch sp* 9 times, then ch 64, turn, starting in second chain from hook, work 63 dc into the chain, sl st into the same ch sp, ch 1, 1 dc in next tr, 1 dc in next ch sp, sl st into first st, cut yarn. (161 dc)
Tie the two shoulder straps together at your desired length and finish the project by sewing in the loose ends.

Beach bag

Crocheted in a gloriously chunky cotton yarn with a macramé shoulder strap, this bag is reassuringly robust. Perfect to shove a towel into and sling over your shoulder when you cycle down to the water's edge for the last swim of the day.

CROCHET HOOK: 12 mm (US P/16 or size to achieve tension)
YARN: 102 m/111½ yd of 4 mm cotton yarn for macramé
YARN A (ORANGE): 46m/50 yd or 230 g/8 oz
YARN B (BROWN): 56m/61 yd or 280 g/10 oz
EQUIPMENT: darning needle, scissors, stitch markers
STITCHES: chain stitch, slip stitch, double crochet, treble crochet, square knot
TENSION (GAUGE): 6.5 sts x 3.5 rows of treble crochet to 10 x 10 cm (4 x 4 in)
SIZE: 32 x 25 cm (12½ x 9¾ in) excluding strap.
CONSTRUCTION: The bag is worked in one piece with an optional colour change and a macramé knotted shoulder strap.
TIPS: Don't worry too much about tension. A bag doesn't need to have exact measurements. But bear in mind that you may need more yarn if you aren't working to the same tension as in the pattern.

METHOD

Using yarn A, ch 5 and join into a ring with a sl st into the first chain.

ROUND 1: ch 2 (counted as 1 tr here and throughout pattern), 10 tr into foundation chain ring, end with a sl st into the top of the second chain. (11 tr)

ROUND 2: ch 2, *2 tr into next space between 2 treble stitches* 11 times, end with a sl st into the top of the second chain. (23 tr)

ROUND 3: ch 2, *1 tr in next space, 2 tr in next space* 11 times, 1 tr into last space, end with a sl st into the top of the second chain. (35 tr)

ROUND 4: ch 2, 1 tr into first space, *2 tr in next space, 1 tr in next two spaces* 11 times, end with a sl st into the top of the second chain. (46 tr)

Start building the mesh of the bag by working in the round in a continuous spiral. It's useful to use a stitch marker to mark the beginning of each round.

ROUND 5: *ch 4, skip 2 sts, 1 dc in next st* 15 times. (15 x 4-ch sps, 15 dc)

ROUND 6: *ch 4, sl st in next 4-ch sp* 15 times. (15 x 4-ch sps, 15 sl sts)

ROUND 7: As round 6. (15 x 4-ch sps, 15 sl sts)

If you want to make the bag in two colours, change colour after round 7.

ROUNDS 8–13: As round 6. (15 x 4-ch sps, 15 sl sts)
ROUND 14: *ch 3, sl st in next 4-ch sp* 15 times. (15 x 3-ch sps, 15 sl sts)
ROUND 15: *ch 3, sl st in next 3-ch sp* 15 times. (15 x 4-ch sps, 15 sl sts)
ROUNDS 16–17: As round 15. (15 x 4-ch sps, 15 sl sts)
ROUND 17: *ch 3, sl st in next 3-ch sp* 15 times. (15 x 4-ch sps, 15 sl sts)
ROUND 18: ch 2 (counts as 1 treble), 1 tr into same stitch, 2 tr in next 3-ch sp 15 times, end with a sl st into the top of the second chain, cut yarn. (32 tr)

Pull the mesh of the bag into place so that all the holes are the same size in both directions. They tend to get a bit wonky while you're working. Sew in the loose ends.

SHOULDER STRAP

Cut 4 lengths of yarn, 2 x 5 metres (5½ yds) and 2 x 2 metres (2¼ yds) long. You need two strands (one of each length) for each side of the bag. Take a strand of each length, fold them both in half, thread them through the edge of the bag and attach them with a lark head's knot, see illustrations 1 to 3. You now have 4 strands to work with.

With the 4 strands in a row, bring the outermost left strand over the two strands in the middle. Place the right-hand strand over the left, then bring it under the centre strands through the loop.

Pull to make a knot. Now repeat the process in the opposite direction. Start again with the 4 strands in a row. This time, bring the outermost right strand over the two strands in the middle. Place the left-hand strand over the right and then bring it under the centre strands through the loop. Pull tight again and you have completed your square knot. Repeat these steps until your shoulder strap is the desired length.

Finish off with a couple of ordinary knots on top of the square knots to keep the shoulder strap from unravelling and cut off the surplus yarn. Repeat the same process for the shoulder strap on the other side. When you have two finished shoulder straps, tie them together with any knot of your choice at the height you want and your bag is ready for adventure!

MACRAMÉ KNOTS FOR SHOULDER STRAP

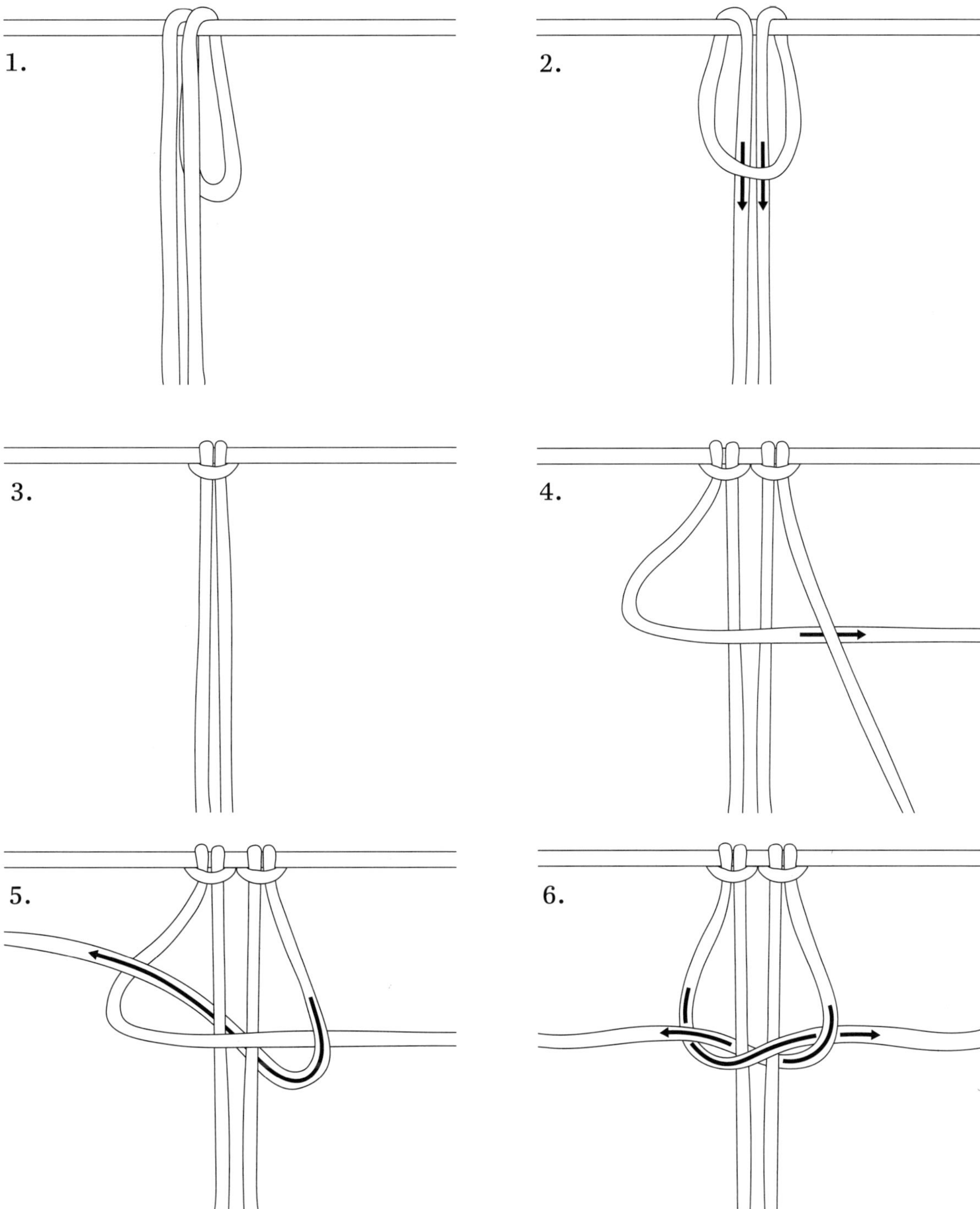

Forager bag

A sturdy bag made from four panels joined together with double crochet. Perfect for transporting all the amazing things you've picked out in the countryside, from wildflowers to this year's apple harvest.

CROCHET HOOK: 7 mm (US K/10½ and above)
YARN: 325 m/355½ yd of 3 mm jute twine
EQUIPMENT: darning needle, scissors
STITCHES: chain stitch, slip stitch, double crochet, treble crochet
TENSION (GAUGE): after row 1, the short sides of the triangle should measure about 5.5 cm (2 in)
SIZE: approx. 45 x 43 cm (17¾ x 17 in) excluding shoulder strap
CONSTRUCTION: The front and back of the bag consist of four granny triangles joined together to create the final shape. You will need 2 triangles of each sort (A and B). The triangles are joined with double crochet and the shoulder strap is made by twisting the jute twine into a rope.

METHOD

TRIANGLE A: 8-row GRANNY TRIANGLE
TRIANGLE B: 12-row GRANNY TRIANGLE

Ch 4 and sl st into first ch to create ring.

ROW 1: ch 4 (counted as 1 tr + 1 ch here and throughout pattern), [3 tr, ch 2, 3 tr, ch 1, 1 tr] into foundation chain ring, turn. (8 tr, 2 x 1-ch sps, 1 x 2-ch sp)

ROW 2: ch 4, 3 tr in next 1-ch sp, ch 1, [3 tr, ch 2, 3 tr] in next 2-ch sp, ch 1, 3 tr in next 1-ch sp, ch1, 1 tr into third ch at start of previous row, turn. (14 tr, 4 x 1-ch sps, 1x 2-ch sp)

ROW 3: ch 4, *3 tr in next 1-ch sp, ch 1* twice, [3 tr, ch 2, 3 tr] in next 2-ch sp, ch 1, *3 tr in next 1-ch sp, ch 1* twice, 1 tr into third ch at start of previous row, turn. (20 tr, 6 x 1-ch sps, 1 x 2-ch sp)

ROW 4: ch 4, *3 tr in next 1-ch sp, ch 1* 3 times, [3 tr, ch 2, 3 tr] in next 2-ch sp, ch 1, *3 tr in next 1-ch sp, ch 1* 3 times, 1 tr into third ch at start of previous row, turn. (26 tr, 8 x 1-ch sps, 1 x 2-ch sp)

ROW 5: ch 4, *3 tr in next 1-ch sp, ch 1* 4 times, [3 tr, ch 2, 3 tr] in next 2-ch sp, ch 1, *3 tr in next 1-ch sp, ch 1* 4 times, 1 tr into third ch at start of previous row, turn. (32 tr, 10 x 1-ch sps, 1 x 2-ch sp)

ROW 6: ch 4, *3 tr in next 1-ch sp, ch 1* 5 times, [3 tr, ch 2, 3 tr] in next 2-ch sp, ch 1, *3 tr in next 1-ch sp, ch 1* 5 times, 1 tr into third ch at start of previous row, turn. (38 tr, 12 x 1-ch sps, 1 x 2-ch sp)

ROW 7: ch 4, *3 tr in next 1-ch sp, ch 1* 6 times, [3 tr, ch 2, 3 tr] in next 2-ch sp, ch 1, *3 tr in next 1-ch sp, ch 1* 6 times, 1 tr into third ch at start of previous row, turn. (44 tr, 14 1-ch sp, 1 2-ch sp)

ROW 8: ch 4, *3 tr in next 1-ch sp, ch 1* 7 times, [3 tr, ch 2, 3 tr] in next 2-ch sp, ch 1, *3 tr in next 1-ch sp, ch 1* 7 times, 1 tr into third ch at start of previous row, turn. (50 tr, 16 x 1-ch sps, 1 x 2-ch sp)

For triangle A, cut yarn after completing row 8 and then work the same pattern again. To make triangle B, keep following the pattern until you have completed row 12.

ROW 9: ch 4, *3 tr in next 1-ch sp, ch 1* 8 times, [3 tr, ch 2, 3 tr] in next 2-ch sp, ch 1, *3 tr in next 1-ch sp, ch 1* 8 times, 1 tr into third ch at start of previous row, turn. (56 tr, 18 x 1-ch sps, 1 x 2-ch sp)

ROW 10: ch 4, *3 tr in next 1-ch sp, ch 1* 9 times, [3 tr, ch 2, 3 tr] in next 2-ch sp, ch 1, *3 tr in next 1-ch sp, ch 1* 9 times, 1 tr into third ch at start of previous row, turn. (62 tr, 20 x 1-ch sps, 1 x 2-ch sp)

ROW 11: ch 4, *3 tr in next 1-ch sp, ch 1* 10 times, [3 tr, ch 2, 3 tr] in next 2-ch sp, ch 1, *3 tr in next 1-ch sp, ch 1* 10 times, 1 tr into third ch at start of previous row, turn. (68 tr, 22 x 1-ch sps, 1 x 2-ch sp)

ROW 12: ch 4, *3 tr in next 1-ch sp, ch 1* 11 times, [3 tr, ch 2, 3 tr] in next 2-ch sp, ch 1, *3 tr in next 1-ch sp, ch 1* 11 times, 1 tr into third ch at start of previous row, cut yarn. (74 tr, 24 x 1-ch sps, 1 x 2-ch sp)

MAKING UP

1. Place the short side of triangle A against the long side of triangle B, join with double crochet to create the shape below. The side with visible double crochet stitches will now be the wrong side. Repeat the same process with the other two triangles.
2. Place the front and back on top of each other, right sides facing and join with double crochet along the outside edge. Add a couple of extra double crochet stitches around the corners to make them more square. Sew in the loose ends with a darning needle.

SHOULDER STRAP

1. Turn the bag inside out and place a weight about 45 cm (17¾ in) away from the centre of the bag. Thread the twine through the top of the bag on one side, over the weight and through the top of the bag on the other side. Repeat this process16 times, cut the twine at the centre of the strap and tie the ends together.
2. Attach the twine slightly above the top edge of the bag and wind it around the 16 strands. It's easiest if you keep the twine wound on its reel or in a ball. Hold the work with both hands and wind tightly. Continue until you reach the opposite side. Finish off by sewing the end of the twine into the work with a darning needle to attach it firmly.

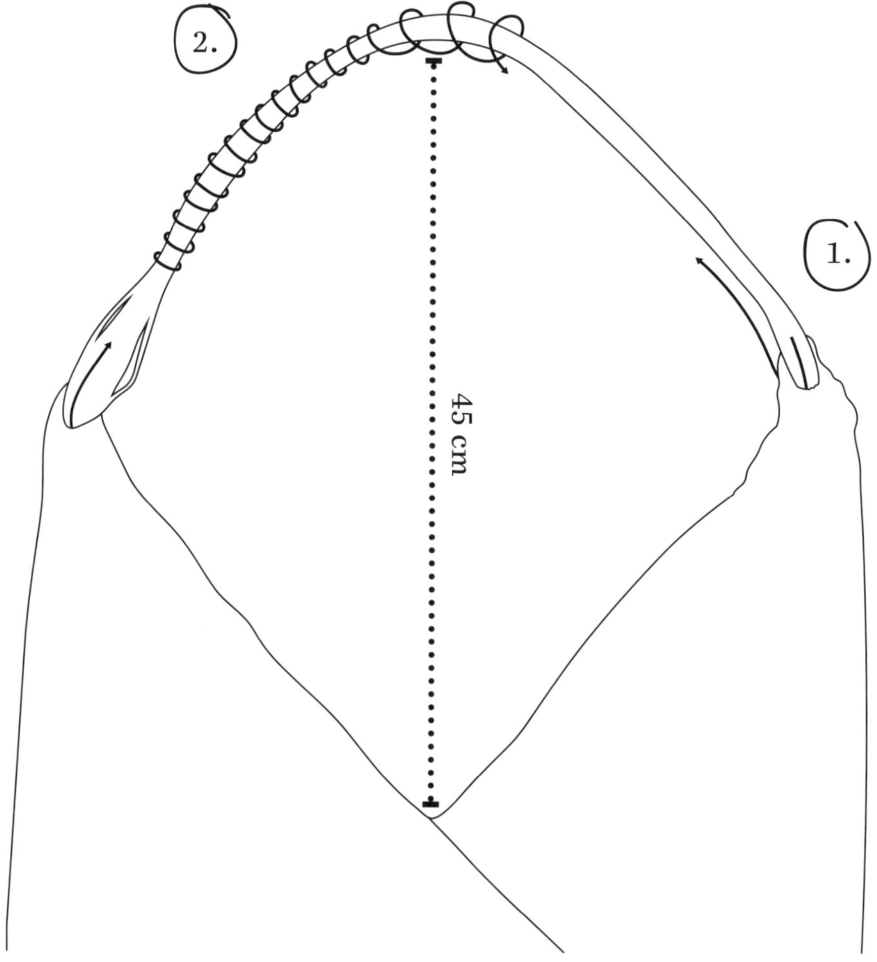

Sunshine hat

A simple, airy design with a wavy brim. The hat is crocheted in one piece, so after 26 rounds of crochet, you'll be able to enjoy the sun, shaded by your new hat, keeping your head cool all summer long.

CROCHET HOOK: 7 mm (US K/10½ and above)

YARN: 2 balls of cotton ribbon yarn, super chunky (super bulky), 125 m/136 yd per 250 g/8¾ oz ball. Amount used: 320 g/11¼ oz

EQUIPMENT: darning needle, scissors

STITCHES: chain stitch, slip stitch, double crochet, treble crochet

TENSION (GAUGE): 11 sts x 11.5 rows to 10 x 10 cm (4 x 4 in)

SIZE: one size, head 54 cm (21¼ in) + stretch, brim 37 cm (14½ in) diameter

CONSTRUCTION: The hat is worked in one piece.

TIPS: Don't worry too much about your tension. A sun hat doesn't need to have exact measurements. But bear in mind that you may need more yarn if you aren't working to the same tension as in the pattern.

Use a stitch marker to mark the first stitch in each new round – it's easy to lose track when you're working in the round.

METHOD

Work 4 ch and join into a ring with a sl st into the first chain.
Worked in the round.

ROUND 1: ch 1 (not counted as a stitch here or throughout pattern), 7 dc into foundation chain ring, sl st into first stitch, pull the end of the yarn tight. (7 dc)

ROUND 2: ch 1, 2 dc in every st, end with a sl st into first st. (14 dc)

ROUND 3: ch 1, *1 dc in next st, 2 dc in next st* 7 times, end with a sl st into first st. (21 dc)

ROUND 4: ch 1, *1 dc in next 2 sts, 2 dc in next st* 7 times, end with a sl st into first st. (28 dc)

ROUND 5: ch 1, *1 dc in next 3 sts, 2 dc in next st* 7 times, end with a sl st into first st. (35 dc)

ROUND 6: ch 1, *1 dc in next 4 sts, 2 dc in next st* 7 times, end with a sl st into first st. (42 dc)

ROUND 7: ch 1, *1 dc in next 5 sts, 2 dc in next st* 6 times, 1 dc in next 6 sts, end with a sl st into first st. (48 dc)

ROUND 8: ch 1, *1 dc in next 20 sts, 2 dc in next st* twice, 1 dc in next 6 sts, end with a sl st into first st. (50 dc)

ROUND 9: ch 1, *1 dc in next 10 sts, 2 dc in next st* 4 times, 1 dc in next 6 sts, end with a sl st into first st. (54 dc)

ROUND 10: ch 1, *1 dc in next 15 sts, 2 dc in next st* 3 times, 1 dc in next 6 sts, end with a sl st into first st. (57 dc)

ROUND 11: ch 1, *1 dc in next 20 sts, 2 dc in next st* twice, 1 dc in next 15 sts, end with a sl st into first st. (59 dc)

ROUND 12: ch 1, 1 dc in every st all the way round, end with a sl st into first st. (59 dc)

ROUNDS 13–14: As round 12. (59 dc)

ROUND 15: ch 3 (counted as 1 st here and throughout pattern), *ch 1, skip 1 st, 1 tr in next st* 29 times, ch 1, end with a sl st into the top of the third chain. (30 tr, 30 x 1-ch sps)

ROUND 16: ch 1, *1 dc in next ch sp, 1 dc in next tr* 29 times, 1 dc into last ch sp, end with a sl st into first st. (59 dc)

ROUND 17: As round 15. (30 tr, 30 x 1-ch sps)

ROUND 18: As round 16. (59 dc)

ROUND 19: ch 1, 1 dc in FLO all the way round, end with a sl st into first st. (59 dc in FLO)

ROUND 20: ch 1, *1 dc in next st, 2 dc in next st* 29 times, end with a sl st into first st. (87 dc)

ROUND 21: ch 1, 1 dc in every st all the way round, end with a sl st into first st. (87 dc)

ROUND 22: ch 3, *ch 1, skip 1 st, 1 tr in next st* 43 times, ch 1, end with a sl st into the top of the third chain. (44 tr)

ROUND 23: ch 1, *2 dc in next ch sp, 1 dc in next tr* 43 times, 1 dc in last ch sp, end with a sl st into first st. (130 dc)

ROUND 24: ch 3 *ch 1, skip 1 st, 1 tr in next st* 64 times, ch 1, end with a sl st into the top of the third chain. (65 tr)

ROUND 25: ch 1, 2 dc in every ch sp all the way round, end with a sl st into first st. (130 dc)

ROUND 26: ch 1, 1 dc in every st all the way round, end with a sl st into first st, cut yarn. (130 dc)
Finish the project by sewing in the loose ends.

Boris beret

Crocheted in one piece in soft, warm wool. A decorative edge and the top in contrasting cotton add a special touch to this beret – a classic with a twist.

CROCHET HOOKS: 9 mm and 7 mm (US N/13 and K/10½ and above)
YARN A: 2 balls of chunky merino wool, super chunky (super bulky), 65 m/71 yd per 100 g/3½ oz ball. Amount used: 125 g/4½ oz
YARN B: 1 ball of cotton ribbon yarn, super chunky (super bulky), 125 m/136 yd per 250 g/8¾ oz ball. Amount used: 15 g/½ oz
EQUIPMENT: darning needle, scissors, stitch markers
STITCHES: chain stitch, slip stitch, double crochet
TENSION (GAUGE): 9.5 sts x 11 rows to 10 x 10 cm (4 x 4 in)
SIZE: 25 cm (21¼ in) in diameter, head size 54 cm (14½ in) + stretch
CONSTRUCTION: The beret is worked in one piece with an optional yarn change.
TIPS: Use a stitch marker to mark the first stitch in each new round because it can be tricky to see where you are when working in the round.

Don't worry too much about your tension. A beret doesn't need to have exact measurements. But bear in mind that you may need more yarn if you aren't working to the same tension as in the pattern.

METHOD

Using a 9 mm (US N/13) crochet hook and yarn A, ch 3 and join into a ring with a sl st into the first chain.

ROUND 1: ch 1 (not counted as a stitch here or throughout pattern), 6 dc into foundation chain ring, end with a sl st into first dc. (6 dc)
ROUND 2: ch 1, 2 dc in every st, end with a sl st into first dc. (12 dc)
ROUND 3: ch 1, *1 dc in next st, 2 dc in next st* 7 times, end with a sl st into first dc. (21 dc)
ROUND 4: ch 1, *1 dc in next 2 sts, 2 dc in next st* 7 times, end with a sl st into first dc. (28 dc)
ROUND 5: ch 1, 28 dc, end with a sl st into first dc. (28 dc)
ROUND 6: ch 1, *1 dc in next 2 sts, 2 dc in next st* 9 times, end with a sl st into first dc. (37 dc)
ROUND 7: ch 1, *1 dc in next 3 sts, 2 dc in next st* 9 times, end with a sl st into first dc. (45 dc)
ROUND 8: ch 1, 45 dc in every st, end with a sl st into first dc. (45 dc)
ROUND 9: ch 1, *1 dc in next 4 sts, 2 dc in next st* 9 times, end with a sl st into first dc. (54 dc)
ROUND 10: ch 1, 54 dc, end with a sl st into first dc. (54 dc)

ROUND 11: ch 1, *1 dc in next 5 sts, 2 dc in next st* 9 times, end with a sl st into first dc. (63 dc)

ROUND 12: ch 1, 63 dc, end with a sl st into first dc. (63 dc)

ROUND 13: ch 1, *1 dc in next 6 sts, 2 dc in next st* 9 times, end with a sl st into first dc. (72 dc)

ROUND 14: ch 1, 72 dc, end with a sl st into first dc. (72 dc)

ROUND 15: ch 1, 72 dc in BLO, end with a sl st into first dc. (72 dc in BLO)

ROUND 16: ch 1, *10 dc, 2 dc tog* 6 times, end with a sl st into first dc. (66 dc)

ROUND 17: ch 1, *20 dc, 2 dc tog* 3 times, end with a sl st into first dc. (63 dc)

ROUND 18: ch 1, *7 dc, 2 dc tog* 7 times, end with a sl st into first dc. (56 dc)

ROUND 19: ch 1, 56 dc, end with a sl st into first dc. (56 dc)

ROUND 20: As round 19. (56 dc)

ROUND 21: ch 1, 56 dc, end with a sl st into first dc, cut yarn A. (56 dc)

Join yarn B into the first st of the previous rounds and change to 7 mm (US K/10½ and above) hook for the last round.

ROUND 22: ch 1, 56 dc in FLO, end with a sl st into first dc, cut yarn B. (56 dc in FLO)

Sew in the loose ends.

MAKING UP

1. Crochet a chain to top off the beret with a loop. Using yarn B, make a slip knot with an extra long tail, ch 7, cut yarn leaving a good length of yarn for the end.
2. Finish off the top of the beret by threading the chain through the little hole in the centre of the beret from the inside to the outside and back again. Sew down the ends inside the beret.

Fisherman's hat

The fisherman's hat is short with a thick folded edge to keep you warm all through the colder months. Here in Sweden, this is an essential winter accessory.

CROCHET HOOK: 9 mm (US N/13)
YARN: 2 balls of British natural wool, super chunky (super bulky), 65 m/71 yd per 100 g/3½ oz ball. Amount used: 175 g/6 oz
EQUIPMENT: darning needle, scissors
STITCHES: chain stitch, slip stitch, double crochet, overcast stitch
TENSION (GAUGE): 11 sts x 12 rows to 10 x 10 cm (4 x 4 in)
SIZE: one size, 46 x 18 cm (18 x 7 in) + stretch with edge folded up
CONSTRUCTION: The hat is worked flat in one piece, joined into a cylinder with double crochet and finally sewn together at the top using overcast stitch.
TIPS: Don't worry too much about tension. A hat doesn't need to have exact measurements and working double crochet only through the back loops makes your crochet quite stretchy. But bear in mind that you may need more yarn if you aren't working to the same tension as in the pattern.

It's a good idea to count your stitches as you go along. The first and last stitches tend to wander off towards the edge and are easily overlooked.

METHOD

ROW 1: ch 29, turn.
ROW 2: 1 dc in second ch from hook, 27 dc, turn. (28 dc)
ROW 3: ch 1 (not counted as a stitch here or throughout pattern), work 8 sl sts in BLO, 20 dc in BLO, turn. (8 sl sts in BLO, 20 dc in BLO) *Don't pull your slip stitches too tight or it will be hard to crochet under them on the next rows.*
ROW 4: ch 1, 28 dc in BLO, turn. (28 dc in BLO)
ROWS 5–45: Repeat rows 3–4 22 more times until you have 45 rows (or your crochet measures about 45 cm (17¾ in) wide at its widest side). Work every odd row as row 3 and every even row as row 4.
ROW 46: *Now join the two short sides with double crochet. Choose the side you think looks best as your right side and make the seam on the wrong side.*
28 dc, cut yarn leaving an extra long tail (approx. 40cm [16 in]) so you can use the tail to sew the top of the hat together. *If you are new to crochet, the two short sides might not be exactly the same length. Don't worry – just try to work your double crochet*

stitches so the sides are as level as you can make them. You might need to add or skip a stitch here or there to make the seam close more evenly.

MAKING UP

1. Thread the long tail through a darning needle and use it to sew the top of the hat closed with overcast stitch, see page 27. Sew the stitches about 1 cm (½ in) apart, starting by sewing loosely until you have stitched all the way round. Then pull the yarn tight to close the top. Fasten off.
2. Turn the hat inside out so the side seam is on the inside. Sew in the remaining loose ends and fold the edge up.

Henrik scarf

A perfectly simple basic accessory, with cool detailing that breaks up the pattern and makes it more interesting. The pattern is easy to personalise by adding in more colours or by changing the length or width. The choice is yours.

CROCHET HOOK: 9 mm (US N/13)
YARN: 5 balls of British natural wool, super chunky (super bulky), 65 m/71 yd per 100 g/3½ oz ball. Amount used: 420 g/15 oz
EQUIPMENT: darning needle, scissors
STITCHES: chain stitch, slip stitch, double crochet
TENSION (GAUGE): 11 sts x 12 rows to 10 x 10 cm (4 x 4 in)
SIZE: one size, 145 x 20 cm (57 x 7¾ in) + stretch
CONSTRUCTION: The scarf is worked in one piece.
TIPS: Don't worry about tension. A scarf doesn't need to have exact measurements. But bear in mind that you may need more yarn if you aren't working to the same tension as in the pattern.

It's easy to change the size of this project. You can change the length by adding more stitches from row 1 and the width depends on the number of rows you crochet before turning the work to the left. In other words, add more rows before row 22 if you want a wider scarf. Remember that this will change the number of stitches when you turn your work to start crocheting along the short side and you will need to add the extra stitches to the instructions for the rest of the pattern.

METHOD

ROW 1: ch 98, turn.
ROW 2: 1 dc in second ch from hook, 96 dc, turn. (97 dc)
ROW 3: ch 1 (not counted as a stitch here or throughout pattern), 97 dc in BLO, turn. (97 dc in BLO)
ROWS 4–21: As row 3. (97 dc in BLO)
ROW 22: ch 1, 97 dc in BLO) (97 dc in BLO)
Instead of turning your work, you are now going to crochet to the left, on top of the short side of the work.
ROW 23: 21 dc in short side, turn. (21 dc)
ROW 24: ch 1, 21 dc in BLO, turn. (21 dc in BLO)
ROWS 25–70: As row 24. (21 dc in BLO)
ROW 71: ch 1, 21 dc in BLO) (21 dc in BLO)
ROW 72: Finish your scarf with a double crochet edge. Instead of turning the work, crochet to the left, start with a row of double crochet along the long side and crochet around the whole edge of the scarf until you get back to the start, add a chain stitch at each of the corners, cut yarn.

Moorit slipover

A great piece for those months of the year when the weather can't make its mind up. Easy to style as a layer over a shirt or under a cardigan, this slipover is as simple to crochet as it is to wear.

CROCHET HOOK: 12 mm (US P/16 or size to achieve tension)
YARN: 4 (5) 6 (6) balls of British natural wool, super chunky (super bulky), 65 m/71 yd per 100 g/3½ oz ball. Amount used: S 375 g/13½ oz, M 455 g/16 oz, L 505 g/18 oz, XL 565 g/20 oz
EQUIPMENT: darning needle, scissors, stitch markers, tape measure
STITCHES: chain stitch, slip stitch, double crochet
TENSION (GAUGE): 8 sts x 7 rows to 10 x 10 cm (4 x 4 in)
SIZE: S–XL, see measurements on page 135
CONSTRUCTION: The slipover is made in two identical pieces which are joined with a double crochet seam.

METHOD

SMALL

ROW 1: ch 36, turn.
ROW 2: 1 dc in second ch from hook, 34 dc, turn. (35 dc)
ROW 3: ch 1 (not counted as a stitch here or throughout pattern), 35 dc in BLO, turn. (35 dc in BLO)
ROWS 4–8: As row 3. (35 dc in BLO)
ROW 9: ch 1, 35 dc in BLO, ch 5, turn. (35 dc in BLO, 5 ch)
ROW 10: 1 dc in second ch from hook, 3 dc, 35 dc in BLO, turn. (4 dc, 35 dc in BLO)
ROW 11: ch 1, 39 dc in BLO, turn. (39 dc in BLO)
ROWS 12–24: As row 11. (39 dc in BLO)
ROW 25: ch 1, 35 dc in BLO, turn. (35 dc in BLO)
ROWS 26–30: As row 25. (35 dc in BLO)
ROW 31: ch 1, 35 dc in BLO, cut yarn. (35 dc in BLO)
Repeat the same instructions once more.

MEDIUM

ROW 1: ch 37, turn.
ROW 2: 1 dc in second ch from hook, 35 dc, turn. (36 dc)
ROW 3: ch 1 (not counted as a stitch here or throughout pattern), 36 dc in BLO, turn. (36 dc in BLO)
ROWS 4–10: As row 3. (36 dc in BLO)
ROW 11: ch 1, 36 dc in BLO, ch 5, turn. (36 dc in BLO, 5 ch)

ROW 12: 1 dc in second ch from hook, 3 dc, 36 dc in BLO, turn. (4 dc, 36 dc in BLO)
ROW 13: ch 1, 40 dc in BLO, turn. (40 dc in BLO)
ROWS 14–26: As row 12. (40 dc in BLO)
ROW 27: ch 1, 36 dc in BLO, turn. (36 dc in BLO)
ROWS 28–35: As row 27. (36 dc in BLO)
ROW 36: ch 1, 36 dc in BLO, cut yarn. (36 dc in BLO)
Repeat the same instructions once more.

LARGE

ROW 1: ch 38, turn.
ROW 2: 1 dc in second ch from hook, 36 dc, turn. (37 dc)
ROW 3: ch 1 (not counted as a stitch here or throughout pattern), 37 dc in BLO, turn. (37 dc in BLO)
ROWS 4–11: As row 3. (37 dc in BLO)
ROW 12: ch 1, 37 dc in BLO, ch 5, turn. (37 dc in BLO, 5 ch)
ROW 13: 1 dc in second ch from hook, 3 dc, 37 dc in BLO, turn. (4 dc, 37 dc in BLO)
ROW 14: ch 1, 41 dc in BLO, turn. (41 dc in BLO)
ROWS 15–29: As row 14. (41 dc in BLO)
ROW 30: ch 1, 37 dc in BLO, turn. (37 dc in BLO)
ROWS 31–38: As row 30. (37 dc in BLO)
ROW 39: ch 1, 37 dc in BLO, cut yarn. (37 dc in BLO)
Repeat the same instructions once more.

X-LARGE

ROW 1: ch 39, turn.
ROW 2: 1 dc in second ch from hook, 37 dc, turn. (38 dc)
ROW 3: ch 1 (not counted as a stitch here or throughout pattern), 38 dc in BLO, turn. (38 dc in BLO)
ROWS 4–13: As row 3. (38 dc in BLO)
ROW 14: ch 1, 38 dc in BLO, ch 5, turn. (38 dc in BLO, 5 ch)
ROW 15: 1 dc in second ch from hook, 3 dc, 38 dc in BLO, turn. (4 dc, 38 dc in BLO)
ROW 16: ch 1, 42 dc in BLO, turn. (42 dc in BLO)
ROWS 17–31: As round 16. (42 dc in BLO)
ROW 32: ch 1, 38 dc in BLO, turn. (38 dc in BLO)
ROWS 33–42: As row 32. (38 dc in BLO)
ROW 43: ch 1, 38 dc in BLO, cut yarn. (38 dc in BLO)
Repeat the same instructions once more.

MAKING UP

The slipover has no right or wrong side so choose the side you think looks best as the right side. Crochet the seams from the wrong side.

1. **SIDE SEAMS:** Place the back and front pieces on top of each other with right sides together. Measure 27 cm (10½ in) down from top edge on both sides for the armhole and mark with a stitch marker. Join yarn at the bottom edge and join the pieces with double crochet. Cut yarn and repeat the same process on the other side. It's useful to work double the dc at the start and the end (at the bottom edge and armhole opening) when joining the pieces together because this is where your garment will get the most wear.
2. **SHOULDER SEAMS:** Join yarn at one side of the shoulder and use double crochet to join the front and back pieces until you get to the top of the neck, cut yarn. Repeat the same process on the other side. Sew in the loose ends.

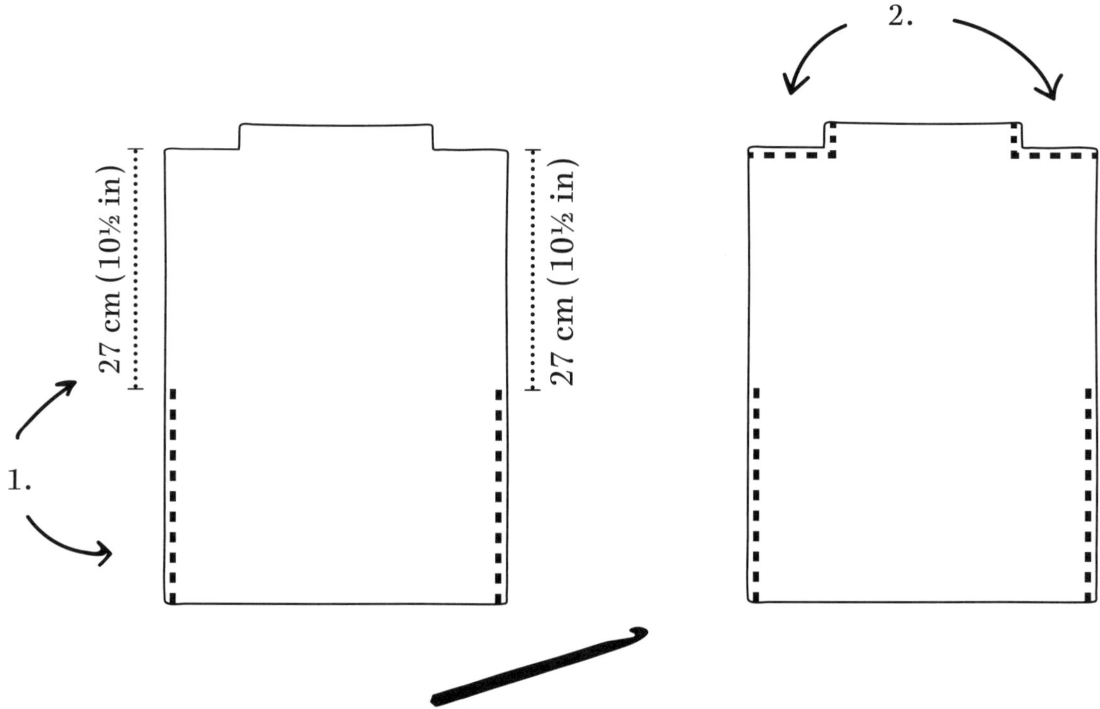

Maiken T-shirt

The Maiken T-shirt is based around a granny square. Its simple construction makes this one of the most rewarding crochet projects in the book – no complications, just Maiken making me feel good!

CROCHET HOOK: 8 mm (US L/11)

YARN: 8 (9) 10 (11) balls of chunky merino wool, super chunky (super bulky), 65 m/71 yd per 100 g/3½ oz ball. Amount used: S 715 g/25¼ oz, M 815 g/28¾ oz, L 915 g/32¼ oz, XL 1,015 g/35¾ oz

EQUIPMENT: darning needle, scissors, stitch markers, tape measure

STITCHES: chain stitch, slip stitch, double crochet, treble crochet

TENSION (GAUGE): after row 1, the square should measure about 6.5 cm (2½ in) square

SIZE: S–XL, see measurements on page 135

CONSTRUCTION: Two granny squares the same size are joined together and then the sleeves are worked downwards in the round.

TIPS: The design is easy to tailor to your individual measurements. Just add or remove rounds to fit. Remember that every round you work will make the t-shirt both longer and wider.

SIZE S, M, L, XL

Crochet in the round (in a square). The side facing you is the right side.

Ch 5 and join into a ring with a sl st into the first chain.

ROUND 1: ch 3 (counted as 1 tr here and throughout pattern), 2 tr into foundation chain ring, ch 2 (this is the first corner). Continue working in the round into the ring to the end of the round, *3 tr, ch 2* 3 times to make 4 groups of 3 trebles (the first group is 3 ch and 2 tr), ending with a sl st into the top of the third chain. (12 tr, 4 x 2-ch sps)

The square should now measure about 6.5 x 6.5 cm (2½ x 2½ in) across. If not, this is a good time to adjust your tension.

ROUND 2: ch 3, *[3 tr, ch 2, 3 tr] in next 2-ch sp* 3 times, [3 tr, ch 2, 2 tr] in next 2-ch sp, end with a sl st into the top of the third chain. (24 tr, 4 x 2-ch sps)

The first three chain stitches make the third treble in the last group of trebles.

ROUND 3: ch 3, 2 tr in the same space (between two groups of trebles), *[3 tr, ch 2, 3 tr] in next 2-ch sp, 3 tr in next space* 3 times, [3 tr, ch 2, 3 tr] in next 2-ch sp, end with a sl st into the top of the third chain. (36 tr, 4 x 2-ch sps)

ROUND 4: ch 3, 3 tr in next space, *[3 tr, ch 2, 3 tr] in next 2-ch sp, 3 tr in next 2 spaces* 3 times, [3 tr, ch 2, 3 tr] in next 2-ch sp, 2 tr in last space, end with a sl st into the top of the third chain. (48 tr, 4 x 2-ch sps)

ROUND 5: ch 3, 2 tr in the same space, 3 tr in next space, *[3 tr, ch 2, 3 tr] in next 2-ch sp, 3 tr in next 3 spaces* 3 times, [3 tr, ch 2, 3 tr] in next 2-ch sp, 3 tr in last space, end with a sl st into the top of the third chain. (60 tr, 4 x 2-ch sps)

ROUND 6: ch 3, 3 tr in next 2 spaces, *[3 tr, ch 2, 3 tr] in next 2-ch sp, 3 tr in next 4 spaces* 3 times, [3 tr, ch 2, 3 tr] in next 2-ch sp, 3 tr in next space, 2 tr in last space, end with a sl st into the top of the third chain.
(72 tr, 4 x 2-ch sps)

ROUND 7: ch 3, 2 tr in the same space, 3 tr in next 2 spaces, *[3 tr, ch 2, 3 tr] in next 2-ch sp, 3 tr in next 5 spaces* 3 times, [3 tr, ch 2, 3 tr] in next 2-ch sp, 3 tr in next 2 spaces, end with a sl st into the top of the third chain. (84 tr, 4 x 2-ch sps)

ROUND 8: ch 3, 3 tr in next 3 spaces, *[3 tr, ch 2, 3 tr in next 2-ch sp, 3 tr] in next 6 spaces* 3 times, [3 tr, ch 2, 3 tr] in next 2-ch sp, 3 tr in next 2 spaces, 2 tr in last space, end with a sl st into the top of the third chain. (96 tr, 4 x 2-ch sps)

ROUND 9: ch 3, 2 tr in the same space, 3 tr in next 3 spaces, *[3 tr, ch 2, 3 tr] in next 2-ch sp, 3 tr in next 7 spaces* 3 times, [3 tr, ch 2, 3 tr] in next 2-ch sp, 3 tr in next 3 spaces, end with a sl st into the top of the third chain. (108 tr, 4 x 2-ch sps)

ROUND 10: ch 3, 3 tr in next 4 spaces, *[3 tr, ch 2, 3 tr] in next 2-ch sp, 3 tr in next 8 spaces* 3 times, [3 tr, ch 2, 3 tr] in next 2-ch sp, 3 tr in next 3 spaces, 2 tr in last space, end with a sl st into the top of the third chain. (120 tr, 4 x 2-ch sps)

ROUND 11: ch 3, 2 tr in same space, 3 tr in next 4 spaces, *[3 tr, ch 2, 3 tr] in next 2-ch sp, 3 tr in next 9 spaces* 3 times, [3 tr, ch 2, 3 tr] in next 2-ch sp, 3 tr in next 4 spaces, end with a sl st into the top of the third chain. (132 tr, 4 x 2-ch sps) *For Small size, cut yarn and start again, working a second identical square. For other sizes, continue:*

ROUND 12: ch 3, 3 tr in next 5 spaces, *[3 tr, ch 2, 3 tr] in next 2-ch sp, 3 tr in next 10 spaces* 3 times, [3 tr, ch 2, 3 tr] in next 2-ch sp, 3 tr in next 4 spaces, 2 tr in last space, end with a sl st into the top of the third chain. (144 tr, 4 x 2-ch sps) *For Medium size, cut yarn and start again, working a second identical square. For other sizes, continue:*

ROUND 13: ch 3, 2 tr in same space, 3 tr in next 5 spaces, *[3 tr, ch 2, 3 tr] in next 2-ch sp, 3 tr in next 11 spaces* 3 times, [3 tr, ch 2, 3 tr] in next 2-ch sp, 3 tr in next 5 spaces, end with a sl st into the top of the third chain. (156 tr, 4 x 2-ch sps) *For Large size, cut yarn and start again, working a second identical square. For other sizes, continue:*

ROUND 14: ch 3, 3 tr in next 6 spaces, *[3 tr, ch 2, 3 tr] in next 2-ch sp, 3 tr in next 12 spaces* 3 times, [3 tr, ch 2, 3 tr] in next 2-ch sp, 3 tr in next 5 spaces, 2 tr in last space, end with a sl st into the top of the third chain. (168 tr, 4 x 2-ch sps)

ROUND 15: ch 3, 2 tr in same space, 3 tr in next 6 spaces, *[3 tr, ch 2, 3 tr] in next 2-ch sp, 3 tr in next 13 spaces* 3 times, [3 tr, ch 2, 3 tr] in next 2-ch sp, 3 tr in next 6 spaces, end with a sl st into the top of the third chain. (180 tr, 4 x 2-ch sps) *For X-Large size, cut yarn and start again, working a second identical square.*

MAKING UP

1. **SHOULDER SEAMS:** Place the two squares on top of each other with right sides together and work seam from the wrong side. Using a tape measure, measure 12 cm (4¾ in) in from sides at each top edge (about three treble groups towards the centre) and mark with stitch markers. Join the shoulder seams you have measured out on each side using double crochet.

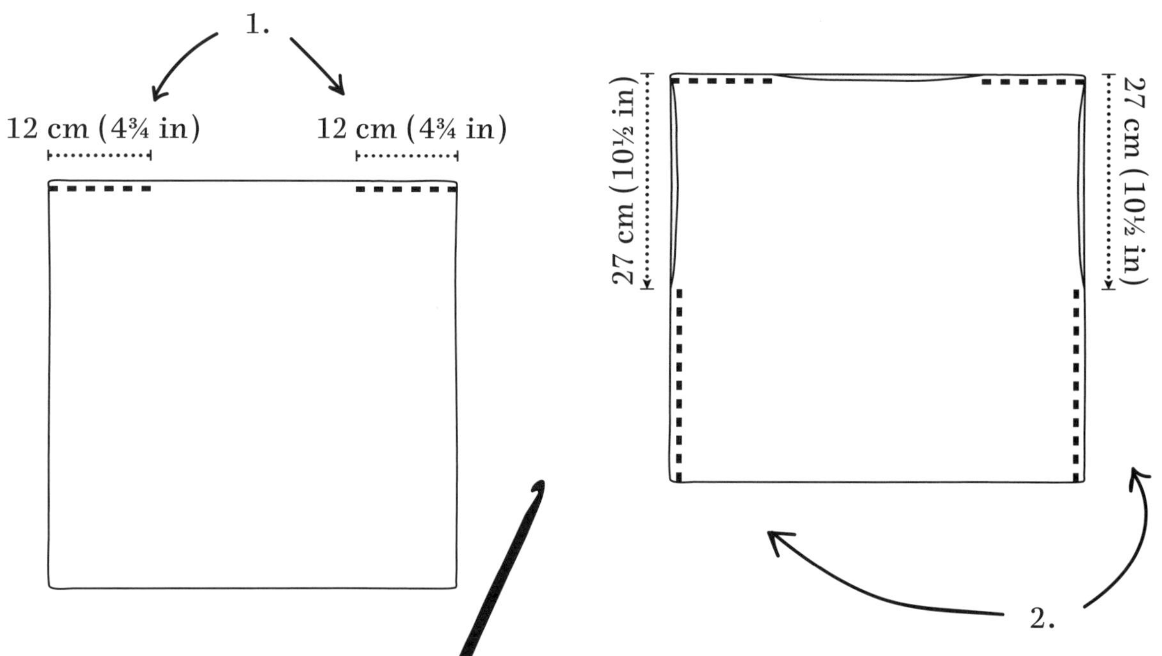

2. **SIDE SEAMS:** Measure 27 cm (10½ in) down from the shoulder seam on each side (about 7 treble groups downwards from the shoulder seam) and mark with stitch markers. Crochet the two sides together from the bottom edge to the stitch markers using double crochet. Repeat the same process on the other side. It's useful to work two dc at the start and the end (at the bottom edge and armhole opening) when joining the sections because this is where your garment will get the most wear.
3. Turn right side out with the seams on the inside. The work will now look like a square with an opening at the top, an opening of 27 cm (10½ in) for each armhole and an open edge at the bottom.

SLEEVES

Now work the sleeves at the armholes on both sides. The instructions are for all sizes. Count the groups of trebles in the armhole opening from the shoulder seam downwards. You should have 14 groups of 3 trebles = 15 spaces.

Join yarn to the 6th group of trebles on one side and work around the armhole as follows:

ROUND 1: ch 3 (counted as 1 tr here and throughout pattern), 2 tr into same space, 3 tr in next 15 spaces, end with a sl st into third chain at start of round. (48 tr)

ROUND 2: ch 3, 3 tr in next 15 spaces, 2 tr into same space as first 3 ch. End with a sl st into third chain at start of round. (48 tr)

ROUNDS 3–6: Repeat rounds 1–2 two more times. (48 tr)

ROUND 7: ch 3, 2 tr into same space, 3 tr in next 15 spaces, end with a sl st into third chain at start of round.

Cut yarn. Sew in the loose ends.

Spring vest

We all need a "throw over any outfit to jazz it up a bit" garment in our wardrobes and this vest does the job perfectly. Its chunky stitches and spontaneous changes of colour will brighten even the greyest of days.

CROCHET HOOK: 12 mm (US P/16 or size to achieve tension)
YARN: 226 m/247 yd of 4 mm cotton yarn for macramé
EQUIPMENT: darning needle, scissors, stitch markers
STITCHES: chain stitch, slip stitch, double crochet
TENSION (GAUGE): 6.5 sts x 7 rows to 10 x 10 cm (4 x 4 in)
SIZE: one size, 60 cm (23½ in) long and 51 cm (20 in) wide
CONSTRUCTION: The vest is worked in one piece and joined at the shoulder seams with double crochet.
TIPS: The perfect project to use up spare yarn.

I changed colour randomly in this design, which often results in unique, abstract colour combinations. I'd like to encourage you to go for it – swap to a new colour whenever you feel like it. If you want your vest to have regular, even stripes, keep using the same colour to the end of the row and change yarn at the start of a new row. If you prefer random stripes – like in my design – change colour wherever you like to produce a beautiful, abstract pattern.

METHOD

ROW 1: ch 63, turn.
ROW 2: 1 dc in second ch from hook, 61 dc, turn. (62 dc)
ROW 3: ch 1 (not counted as a stitch here or throughout pattern), 62 dc, turn. (62 dc)
ROWS 4–19: As row 3. (62 dc)

Now you will divide the work to work the first side section.

ROW 20: ch 1, 15 dc, turn. (15 dc)
ROW 21: ch 1, skip first st, 14 dc, turn. (14 dc)
ROW 22: ch 1, 12 dc, 2 dc tog over next 2 sts, turn. (13 dc)
ROW 23: ch 1, skip first st, 12 dc, turn. (12 dc)
ROW 24: ch 1, 10 dc, 2 dc tog over next 2 sts, turn. (11 dc)
ROW 25: ch 1, skip first st, 10 dc, turn. (10 dc)
ROW 26: ch 1, 8 dc, 2 dc tog over next 2 sts, turn. (9 dc)
ROW 27: ch 1, skip first st, 8 dc, turn. (8 dc)
ROW 28: ch 1, 6 dc, 2 dc tog over next 2 sts, turn. (7 dc)
ROW 29: ch 1, 7 dc, turn. (7 dc)
ROW 30: ch 1, skip first st, 6 dc, turn. (6 dc)
ROW 31: ch 1, 6 dc, turn. (6 dc)

ROWS 32–36: As row 31. (6 dc)
ROW 37: ch 1, 6 dc, ch 1, cut yarn. (6 dc)

BACK

Join yarn one stitch away from the finished side section, leaving one stitch empty between front and back.

ROW 20: ch 1, 30 dc, turn. (30 dc)
ROW 21: ch 1, 5 dc, 2 dc tog, *7 dc, 2 dc tog* twice, 5 dc, turn. (27 dc)
ROW 22: ch 1, 2 dc tog over first and second st, 23 dc, 2 dc tog over last two sts, turn. (25 dc)
ROW 23: ch 1, 2 dc tog over first and second st, 21 dc, 2 dc tog over last two sts, turn. (23 dc)
ROW 24: ch 1, 2 dc tog over first and second st, 19 dc, 2 dc tog over last two sts, turn. (21 dc)
ROW 25: ch 1, 21 dc, turn. (21 dc)
ROWS 26–34: As row 25. (21 dc)
ROW 35: ch 1, 2 dc in first st, 19 dc, 2 dc in last st, turn. (23 dc)
ROW 36: ch 1, 23 dc, turn. (23 dc)
ROW 37: As row 36. (23 dc)
ROW 38: ch 1, 7 dc, 9 sl st, ch 1 and 1 dc in same st, 6 dc, turn. (14 dc)
ROW 39: ch 1, 5 dc, 2 dc tog over last two sts, cut yarn. (6 dc)
Rejoin yarn on opposite side of back and work the other shoulder so both sides of the back are the same: ch 1, 1 dc in same st, 4 dc, 2 dc tog, turn. Cut yarn. (6 dc)

SECOND SIDE PANEL

Rejoin yarn one st in from the finished back section to finally work the second side panel.

ROUND 20: ch 1, 15 dc, turn. (15 dc)
ROUND 21: ch 1, 13 dc, 2 dc tog over last 2 sts, turn. (14 dc)
ROW 22: ch 1, skip first st, 13 dc, turn. (13 dc)
ROW 23: ch 1, 11 dc, 2 dc tog over last 2 sts, turn. (12 dc)
ROW 24: ch 1, skip first st, 11 dc, turn. (11 dc)
ROW 25: ch 1, 9 dc, 2 dc tog over last 2 sts, turn. (10 dc)
ROW 26: ch 1, skip first st, 9 dc, turn. (9 dc)
ROW 27: ch 1, 7 dc, 2 dc tog over last 2 sts, turn. (8 dc)

ROW 28: ch 1, skip first st, 7 dc, turn. (7 dc)
ROW 29: ch 1, 7 dc, turn. (7 dc)
ROW 30: ch 1, skip first st, 6 dc, turn. (6 dc)
ROW 31: ch 1, 6 dc, turn. (6 dc)
ROWS 32–36: As row 31. (6 dc)
ROW 37: ch 1, 6 dc, cut yarn. (6 dc)

MAKING UP

This design has no right or wrong side so choose the side you like best as the right side and crochet the seam from the other side.

1. **SHOULDER SEAMS:** Fold the side panels over the back and join the shoulder seams using double crochet.
2. **ARMHOLES:** Join yarn and work one round of double crochet around each armhole. This will neaten and straighten the edge. I chose to leave the edges raw at the front of my vest but you can work a double crochet row to neaten those edges too.

VISIBLE ENDS

For this vest, I chose to sew the ends in a little and then tie them off so the ends are visible on the right side. I fan the ends out with my fingers to make little tufts. This is a playful but optional way to finish your vest.

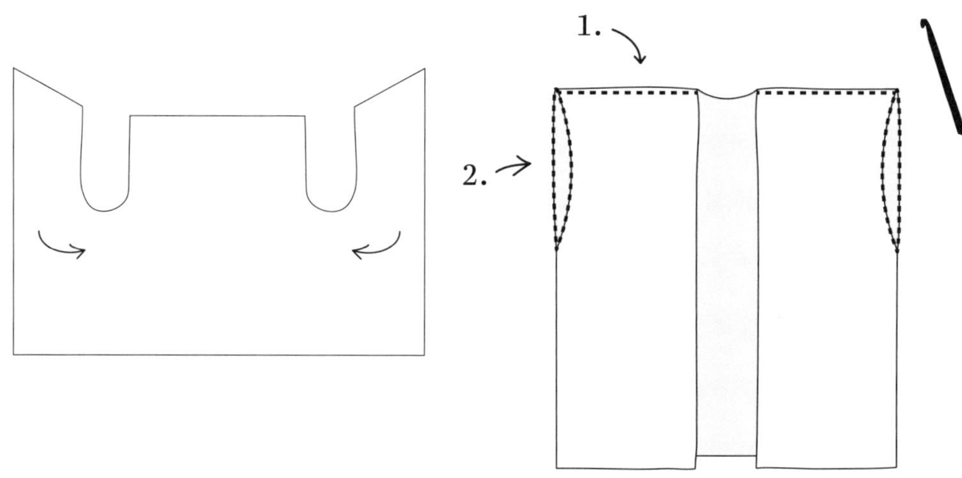

Forest cardigan

Your favourite cardigan. This project is a bit more time-consuming than the others but it's well worth the effort – and most of all, it's a garment to be proud of. The oversized cut and wide sleeves will make this cardigan the best crocheted piece in your wardrobe.

CROCHET HOOK: 9 mm (US N/13)
YARN: 11 (11) 12 (13) balls of chunky merino wool, super chunky (super bulky), 65 m/71 yd per 100 g/3½ oz ball. Amount used: S 1,030 g/36½ oz, M 1,100 g/39 oz, L 1,170 g/41½ oz, XL 1,240 g/43¾ oz
EQUIPMENT: darning needle, scissors, stitch markers
STITCHES: chain stitch, slip stitch, double crochet, treble crochet
TENSION (GAUGE): 11 sts x 10 rows worked in dc in BLO and 4.5 sts x 4.5 sts worked in treble crochet to 10 x 10 cm (4 x 4 in)
SIZE: S–XL, see measurements on page 135
CONSTRUCTION: The main part of the cardigan is worked in one piece. Start by working the rib section, then turn work to the left and work the rest of the cardigan along the long side of the rib. The sleeves are the same for all sizes (S–XL). They are worked separately and are joined to the rest of the cardigan using double crochet.
TIPS: The cardigan is oversized so check the measurements on page 135 before choosing your size.

I combined the wool yarn with a thinner yarn to produce an interesting texture but you can make this just using the wool yarn.

METHOD

SMALL

ROW 1: ch 11, turn.
ROW 2: 1 dc in second ch from hook, 9 dc, turn. (10 dc)
ROW 3: ch 1 (not counted as a stitch here or throughout pattern), 10 dc in BLO, turn. (10 dc in BLO)
ROWS 4–81: As row 3. (10 dc in BLO)
ROW 82: ch 1, 10 dc in BLO, turn work to the left. (10 dc in BLO)
You will now start crocheting along the long side of the work. Crochet into the sides of the previous rows.
ROW 83: ch 3 (counted as 1 tr here and throughout pattern), 1 tr into same row, *skip 1 row, 2 tr in each of next 3 rows, skip 1 row, 2 tr in next row* 13 times, skip next row, 2 tr in next row, 1 tr into last row, turn. (109 tr)

ROW 84: ch 3, 1 tr into same st, *skip 1 st, 2 tr in next st* 53 times, skip 1 st, end with 1 tr into third chain at start of row, turn. (109 tr)

ROWS 85–93: As row 84. (109 tr)

Place two stitch markers 29 sts from the edge of each side of the work to mark where you will work the back.

FIRST SIDE PANEL

Divide work to crochet the first side panel.

ROW 94: ch 3, 1 tr into same st, *skip 1 st, 2 tr in next st* 12 times, turn. (26 tr)

ROW 95: ch 3, *skip 1 st, 2 tr in next st* 12 times, skip 1 st, 1 tr into third chain at start of round, turn. (26 tr)

ROW 96: ch 3, 1 tr into same st, *skip 1 st, 2 tr in next st* 11 times, skip 1 st, 1 tr in next st, 1 tr into third chain at start of round, turn. (26 tr)

ROWS 97–102: Repeat rows 95–96 three times. (26 tr)

ROW 103: ch 3, *skip 1 st, 2 tr in next st* 12 times, skip 1 st, 1 tr into third chain at start of round, cut yarn. (26 tr)

BACK

Join yarn in stitch marked with a stitch marker to the side of the panel you just worked.

ROW 94: ch 3, 1 tr into same st, *skip 1 st, 2 tr in next st* 26 times, turn. (54 tr)

Place a stitch marker 4 sts away from the finished row. This will make it easier when you crochet the other side panel.

ROW 95: ch 3, *skip 1 st, 2 tr in next st* 26 times, skip 1 st, 1 tr into third chain at start of round, turn. (54 tr)

ROW 96: ch 3, 1 tr into same st, *skip 1 st, 2 tr in next st* 25 times, skip 1 st, 1 tr in next st, 1 tr into third chain at start of round, turn. (54 tr)

ROWS 97–100: Repeat rows 95–96 twice more. (54 tr)

ROW 101: ch 3, *skip 1 st, 2 tr in next st* 26 times, skip 1 st, 1 tr into third chain at start of round, cut yarn. (54 tr)

SECOND SIDE PANEL

Join yarn in the stitch marked with the stitch marker 4 sts away from the back and start to crochet working away from the back.

ROW 94: ch 3, 1 tr into same st, *skip 1 st, 2 tr in next st* 11 times, skip 1 st, 1 tr into third chain at start of round, turn. (26 tr)

ROW 95: ch 3, *skip 1 st, 2 tr in next st* 12 times, skip 1 st, 1 tr into third chain at start of round, turn. (26 tr)

ROW 96: ch 3, 1 tr into same st, *skip 1 st, 2 tr in next st* 11 times, skip 1 st, 1 tr in next st, 1 tr into third chain at start of round, turn. (26 tr)

ROWS 97–102: Repeat rows 95–96 three times. (26 tr)

ROW 103: ch 3, *skip 1 st, 2 tr in next st* 12 times, skip 1 st, 1 tr into third chain at start of round, cut yarn. (26 tr)

MEDIUM

ROW 1: ch 11, turn.

ROW 2: 1 dc in second ch from hook, 9 dc, turn. (10 dc)

ROW 3: ch 1 (not counted as a stitch here or throughout pattern), 10 dc in BLO, turn. (10 dc in BLO)

ROWS 4–87: As row 3. (10 dc in BLO)

ROW 88: ch 1, 10 dc in BLO, turn work to the left. (10 dc in BLO)
You will now start crocheting along the long side of the work. Crochet into the side of the previous rows.

ROW 89: ch3 (counted as 1 tr here and throughout whole pattern, 1 tr into same row, *skip 1 row, 2 tr in each of next 3 rows, skip 1 row, 2 tr in next row* 14 times, skip next row, 2 tr into next row, 1 tr into last row, turn. (117 tr)

ROW 90: ch 3, 1 tr into same st, *skip 1 st, 2 tr in next st* 57 times, skip 1 st, end with 1 tr into third chain at start of round, turn. (117 tr)

ROWS 91–99: As row 90. (117 tr)
Place two stitch markers 31 sts from the edge at both sides of work to show where you will work the back.

FIRST SIDE PANEL

Divide work to crochet the first side panel.

ROW 100: ch 3, 1 tr into same st, *skip 1 st, 2 tr in next st* 13 times, turn. (28 tr)

ROW 101: ch 3, *skip 1 st, 2 tr in next st* 13 times, skip 1 st, 1 tr into third chain at start of round, turn. (28 tr)

ROW 102: ch 3, 1 tr into same st, *skip 1 st, 2 tr in next st* 12 times, skip 1 st, 1 tr in next st, 1 tr into third chain at start of round, turn. (28 tr)

ROWS 103–108: Repeat rows 101–102 three more times. (28 tr)

ROW 109: ch 3, *skip 1 st, 2 tr in next st* 13 times, skip 1 st, 1 tr into third chain at start of round, cut yarn. (28 tr)

BACK

Join yarn in stitch marked with a stitch marker to the side of the panel you just worked.

ROW 100: ch 3, 1 tr into same st, *skip 1 st, 2 tr in next st* 28 times, turn. (58 tr) *Place a stitch marker 4 sts away from the finished row. This will make it easier when you crochet the other side panel.*

ROW 101: ch 3, *skip 1 st, 2 tr in next st* 28 times, skip 1 st, 1 tr into third chain at start of round, turn. (58 tr)

ROW 102: ch 3, 1 tr into same st, *skip 1 st, 2 tr in next st* 27 times, skip 1 st, 1 tr in next st, 1 tr into third chain at start of round, turn. (58 tr)

ROWS 103–106: Repeat rows 101–102 two more times. (58 tr)

ROW 107: ch 3, *skip 1 st, 2 tr in next st* 28 times, skip 1 st, 1 tr into third chain at start of round, cut yarn. (58 tr)

SECOND SIDE PANEL

Join yarn in the stitch marked with the stitch marker 4 sts away from the back and start to crochet working away from the back.

ROW 100: ch 3, 1 tr into same st, *skip 1 st, 2 tr in next st* 12 times, skip 1 st, 1 tr into third chain at start of round, turn. (28 tr)

ROW 101: ch 3, *skip 1 st, 2 tr in next st* 13 times, skip 1 st, 1 tr into third chain at start of round, turn. (28 tr)

ROW 102: ch 3, 1 tr into same st, *skip 1 st, 2 tr in next st* 12 times, skip 1 st, 1 tr in next st, 1 tr into third chain at start of round, turn. (28 tr)

ROWS 103–108: Repeat rows 101–102 three more times. (28 tr)

ROW 109: ch 3, *skip 1 st, 2 tr in next st* 13 times, skip 1 st, 1 tr into third chain at start of round, cut yarn. (28 tr)

LARGE

ROW 1: ch 11, turn.

ROW 2: 1 dc in second ch from hook, 9 dc, turn. (10 dc)

ROW 3: ch 1 (not counted as a stitch here or throughout pattern), 10 dc in BLO, turn. (10 dc in BLO)

ROWS 4–93: As row 3. (10 dc in BLO)

ROW 94: ch 1, 10 dc in BLO, turn work to the left. (10 dc in BLO)
You will now start crocheting along the long side of the work. Crochet into the side of the previous rows.

ROW 95: ch3 (counted as 1 tr here and throughout whole pattern, 1 tr into same row, *skip 1 row, 2 tr in each of next 3 rows, skip 1 row, 2 tr into next row* 15 times, skip next row, 2 tr into next row, 1 tr into last row, turn. (125 tr)

ROW 96: ch 3, 1 tr into same st, *skip 1 st, 2 tr in next st* 61 times, skip 1 st, end with 1 tr into third chain at start of round, turn. (125 tr)

ROWS 97–105: As row 96. (125 tr)
Place 2 stitch markers 33 sts from the edge at both sides of work to mark where the back will be worked.

FIRST SIDE PANEL

Divide work to crochet the first side panel.

ROW 106: ch 3, 1 tr into same st, *skip 1 st, 2 tr in next st* 14 times, turn. (30 tr)

ROW 107: ch 3, *skip 1 st, 2 tr in next st* 14 times, skip 1 st, 1 tr into third chain at start of round, turn. (30 tr)

ROW 108: ch 3, 1 tr into same st, *skip 1 st, 2 tr in next st* 13 times, skip 1 st, 1 tr in next st, 1 tr into third chain at start of round, turn. (30 tr)

ROWS 109–114: Repeat rows 107–108 three more times. (32 tr)

ROW 115: ch 3, *skip 1 st, 2 tr in next st* 14 times, skip 1 st, 1 tr into third chain at start of round, cut yarn. (32 tr)

BACK

Join yarn in stitch marked with a stitch marker to the side of the panel you just worked.

ROW 106: ch 3, 1 tr into same st, *skip 1 st, 2 tr in next st* 30 times, turn. (62 tr)

Place a stitch marker 4 sts away from the finished row. This will make it easier when you crochet the other side panel.

ROW 107: ch 3, *skip 1 st, 2 tr in next st* 30 times, skip 1 st, 1 tr into third chain at start of round, turn. (62 tr)

ROW 108: ch 3, 1 tr into same st, *skip 1 st, 2 tr in next st* 29 times, skip 1 st, 1 tr in next st, 1 tr into third chain at start of round, turn. (62 tr)

ROWS 109–112: Repeat rows 107–108 two more times. (62 tr)

ROW 113: ch 3, *skip 1 st, 2 tr in next st* 30 times, skip 1 st, 1 tr into third chain at start of round, cut yarn. (62 tr)

SECOND SIDE PANEL

Join yarn in the stitch marked with the stitch marker 4 sts away from the back and start to crochet working away from the back.

ROW 106: ch 3, 1 tr into same st, *skip 1 st, 2 tr in next st* 13 times, skip 1 st, 1 tr into third chain at start of round, turn. (30 tr)

ROW 107: ch 3, *skip 1 st, 2 tr in next st* 14 times, skip 1 st, 1 tr into third chain at start of round, turn. (30 tr)

ROW 108: ch 3, 1 tr into same st, *skip 1 st, 2 tr in next st* 13 times, skip 1 st, 1 tr in next st, 1 tr into third chain at start of round, turn. (30 tr)

ROWS 109–114: Repeat rows 107–108 three more times. (30 tr)

ROW 115: ch 3, *skip 1 st, 2 tr in next st* 14 times, skip 1 st, 1 tr into third chain at start of round, cut yarn. (30 tr)

X-LARGE

ROW 1: ch 11, turn.

ROW 2: 1 dc in second ch from hook, 9 dc, turn. (10 dc)

ROW 3: ch 1 (not counted as a stitch here or throughout pattern), 10 dc in BLO, turn. (10 dc in BLO)

ROWS 4–99: As row 3. (10 dc in BLO)

ROW 100: ch 1, 10 dc in BLO, turn work to the left. (10 dc in BLO)
You will now start crocheting along the long side of the work. Crochet into the side of the previous rows.

ROW 101: ch 3 (counted as 1 tr here and throughout whole pattern), 1 tr into same row, *skip 1 row, 2 tr in each of next 3 rows, skip 1 row, 2 tr into next row* 16 times, skip next row, 2 tr into next row, 1 tr into last row, turn. (133 tr)

ROW 102: ch 3, 1 tr into same st, *skip 1 st, 2 tr in next st* 65 times, skip 1 st, end with 1 tr into third chain at start of round, turn. (133 tr)

ROWS 103–111: As row 102. (133 tr)
Place 2 stitch markers 35 sts from the edge at both sides of work to mark where the back will be worked.

FIRST SIDE PANEL

Divide work to crochet the first side panel.

ROW 112: ch 3, 1 tr into same st, *skip 1 st, 2 tr in next st* 15 times, turn. (32 tr)

ROW 113: ch 3, *skip 1 st, 2 tr in next st* 15 times, skip 1 st, 1 tr into third chain at start of round, turn. (32 tr)

ROW 114: ch 3, 1 tr into same st, *skip 1 st, 2 tr in next st* 14 times, skip 1 st, 1 tr in next st, 1 tr into third chain at start of round, turn. (32 tr)

ROWS 115–120: Repeat rows 113–114 three more times. (32 tr)

ROW 121: ch 3, *skip 1 st, 2 tr in next st* 15 times, skip 1 st, 1 tr into third chain at start of round, cut yarn. (32 tr)

BACK

Join yarn in stitch marked with a stitch marker to the side of the panel you just worked.

ROW 112: ch 3, 1 tr into same st, *skip 1 st, 2 tr in next st* 32 times, turn. (66 tr) *Place a stitch marker 4 sts away from the finished row. This will make it easier when you crochet the other side panel.*

ROW 113: ch 3, *skip 1 st, 2 tr in next st* 32 times, skip 1 st, 1 tr into third chain at start of round, turn. (66 tr)

ROW 114: ch 3, 1 tr into same st, *skip 1 st, 2 tr in next st* 31 times, skip 1 st, 1 tr in next st, 1 tr into third chain at start of round, turn. (66 tr)

ROWS 115–118: Repeat rows 113–114 two more times. (66 tr)

ROW 119: ch 3, *skip 1 st, 2 tr in next st* 32 times, skip 1 st, 1 tr into third chain at start of round, cut yarn. (66 tr)

SECOND SIDE PANEL

Join yarn in the stitch marked with the stitch marker 4 sts away from the back and start to crochet working away from the back.

ROW 112: ch 3, 1 tr into same st, *skip 1 st, 2 tr in next st* 14 times, skip 1 st, 1 tr into third chain at start of round, turn. (32 tr)

ROW 113: ch 3, *skip 1 st, 2 tr in next st* 15 times, skip 1 st, 1 tr into third chain at start of round, turn. (32 tr)

ROW 114: ch 3, 1 tr into same st, *skip 1 st, 2 tr in next st* 14 times, skip 1 st, 1 tr in next st, 1 tr into third chain at start of round, turn. (32 tr)

ROWS 115–120: Repeat rows 113–114 three more times. (32 tr)

ROW 121: ch 3, *skip 1 st, 2 tr in next st* 15 times, skip 1 st, 1 tr into third chain at start of round, cut yarn. (32 tr)

SLEEVES

The sleeves are the same for all sizes.

ROW 1: ch 13, turn.
ROW 2: 1 dc in second ch from hook, 11 dc, turn. (12 dc)
ROW 3: ch 1, 12 dc in BLO, turn. (12 dc in BLO)
ROWS 4–20: As row 3. (12 dc in BLO)
ROW 21: ch 1, fold work in half and join the two ends with 12 dc. (12 dc)
Now start to work the long edge of the crocheted hoop, working in the round. Crochet into the side of the previous rows. Numbering of rows/rounds continues consecutively.
ROUND 22: ch 3, 1 tr into next row, 2 tr into next 18 rows, 1 tr into last row, sl st into the top of the third chain. (39 tr)
ROUND 23: ch 3, 1 tr into same st, 2 tr in next st, skip 1 st, 2 tr in next st* 18 times, sl st into the top of the third chain. (40 tr)
ROUND 24: As round 23. (40 tr)
ROUND 25: ch 3, *skip 1 st, 2 tr in next st* 19 times, skip 1 st, 1 tr into same st as the first 3 chains, sl st into the top of the third chain. (40 tr)
ROUND 26: ch 3, 1 tr in next st, *skip 1 st, 2 tr in next st* 19 times, sl st into the top of the third chain. (40 tr)
ROUNDS 27–34: Repeat rounds 25–26 four more times. (40 tr)
ROW 35: ch 3, *skip 1 st, 2 tr in next st* 19 times, skip 1 st, 1 tr into same st as the first 3 chains, sl st into the top of the third chain. (40 tr)
Your cardigan will need two sleeves so repeat the sleeve pattern once more.

MAKING UP

The cardigan has no right or wrong side so choose the side you like best as the right side and work the seams from the other side.

1. **SHOULDER SEAMS:** Fold the side panels on top of the back, with right sides together. Join yarn and crochet the side panels and back together using double crochet. You will now have some empty stitches in the middle which form the neck.
2. **SLEEVES:** Attach the sleeves to each side of the cardigan using double crochet. Sew in the loose ends.

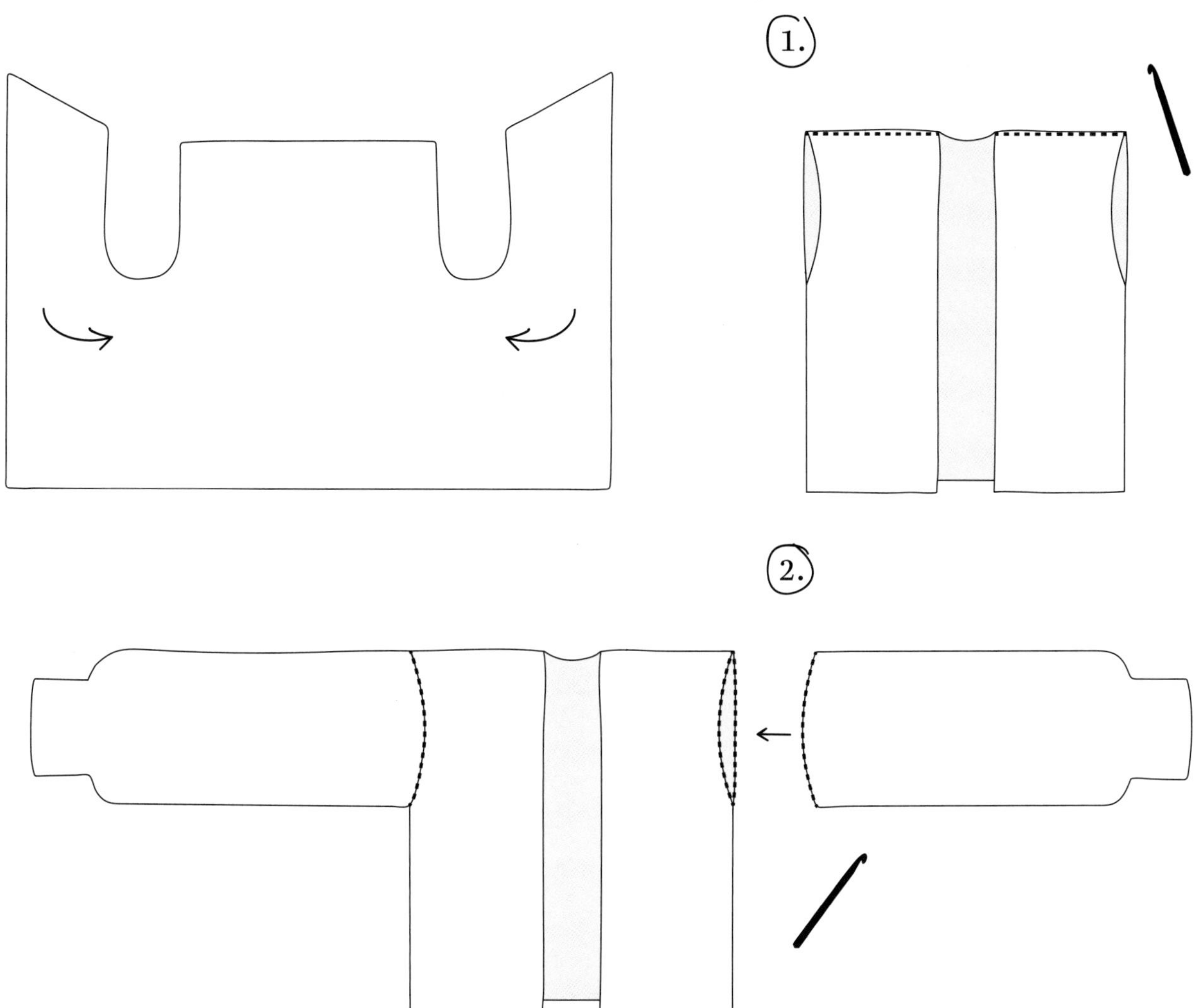
1.
2.

Cylindrical cushion cover

This long, narrow cushion cover is worked in three sections with four crocheted ties to hold it together. Once you have completed the three sections, you sew them together with mattress stitch and, as if by magic, your cushion cover is ready for a cosy night on the sofa or reading in bed.

CROCHET HOOK: 9 mm (US N/13)
YARN: chunky merino wool, super chunky (super bulky), 65 m/71 yd per 100 g/3½ oz ball
COLOUR A (BROWN): 3 balls. Amount used: 250 g/9 oz
COLOUR B (WHITE): 3 balls. Amount used: 205 g/7¼ oz
EQUIPMENT: darning needle, scissors, sewing thread
STITCHES: chain stitch, slip stitch, double crochet, treble crochet, mattress stitch
TENSION (GAUGE): 10 sts x 12 rows worked in double crochet and 9 sts x 4.5 sts worked in treble crochet to 10 x 10 cm (4 x 4 in)
MEASUREMENTS: 18 x 55 cm (7 x 21¾ in)
CONSTRUCTION: The cushion is worked in three sections sewn together using mattress stitch. You will need a cylindrical inner cushion pad measuring 18 x 55 cm (7 x 21¾ in).

METHOD

END SECTION

Start working with yarn A: Ch 3 and sl st into first ch to create ring. Work in the round.

ROUND 1: ch 3 (counted as 1 tr here and throughout pattern), 11 tr into foundation chain ring, end with a sl st into the top of the third chain. (12 tr)

ROUND 2: ch 3, *2 tr into same st* 11 times, 1 tr in last st, end with a sl st into the top of the third chain. (24 tr)

ROUND 3: ch 3, 2 tr in first st, 1 tr in next st *2 tr in next st, 1 tr in next st* 10 times, 1 tr in last st, end with a sl st into the top of the third chain. (35 tr)

ROUND 4: ch 3, 2 tr in first st, 1 tr in next 2 sts *2 tr in next st, 1 tr in next 2 sts* 10 times, 2 tr in last st, end with a sl st into the top of the third chain. (47 tr)

ROUND 5: ch 3, 46 tr in BLO, end with a sl st into the top of the third chain. (47 tr)

ROUND 6: ch 3, 46 tr, end with a sl st into the top of the third chain. (47 tr)

ROUNDS 7–8: As round 6. (47 tr)

ROUND 9: ch 3, 46 tr, end with a sl st into the top of the third chain, cut yarn. (47 tr)

Join colour B in first st in previous round. From round 10 onwards, work back and forth in rows instead of in the round. Numbering of rows/rounds continues consecutively.

ROW 10: ch 1 (not counted as a stitch here or throughout pattern), 1 dc in same st, 46 dc, turn. (47 dc)
ROW 11: ch 1, 47 dc, turn. (47 dc)
ROW 12: As row 11. (47 dc)
ROW 13: ch 1, 47 dc, ch 16, turn. (47 dc, 16 ch)
ROW 14: 1 dc in second ch from hook, 1 dc in next 14 ch, 47 dc, ch 16, turn. (62 dc, 16 ch)
ROW 15: 1 dc in second ch from hook, 1 dc in next 14 ch, 47 dc, turn. (62 dc)
ROW 16: ch 1, 47 dc, turn. (47 dc)
ROWS 17–21: As row 16. (47 dc)
ROW 22: ch 1, 47 dc, cut yarn. (47 dc)

Start again from the start of the pattern and make another piece for the other end of the cushion. When you have made two end sections, start to work the centre of the cushion cover.

CENTRE SECTION

The centre of the cushion cover is worked in rows in yarn A.

ROW 1: ch 48, turn.
ROW 2: 1 dc in second ch from hook, 46 dc, ch 16, turn. (47 dc, 16 ch)
ROW 3: 1 dc in second ch from hook, 1 dc in next 14 ch, 47 dc, ch 16, turn. (62 dc, 16 ch)
ROW 4: 1 dc in second ch from hook, 1 dc in next 14 ch, 47 dc, turn. (62 dc)
ROW 5: ch 1, 47 dc, turn. (47 dc)
ROW 6: ch 3, 46 tr, turn. (47 tr)
ROW 7: ch 1, 46 dc, 1 tr into third chain at start of previous row, turn. (47 dc)
ROW 8: ch 3, 46 tr, turn. (47 tr)
ROW 9: ch 1, 47 dc, turn. (47 dc)
ROW 10: ch 3, 46 tr, turn. (47 tr)
ROW 11: ch 1, 47 dc, turn. (47 dc)
ROW 12: ch 3, 46 tr, turn. (47 tr)
ROW 13: ch 1, 47 dc, ch 16, turn. (47 dc, 16 ch)
ROW 14: 1 dc in second ch from hook, 1 dc in next 14 ch, 47 dc, ch 16, turn. (62 dc, 16 ch)

ROW 15: 1 dc in second ch from hook, 1 dc in next 14 ch, 47 dc, turn. (62 dc)

ROW 16: ch 1, 47 dc, cut yarn. (47 dc)

MAKING UP

Sew the three sections together as shown in the illustration below. Use mattress stitch, see instructions on page 27.

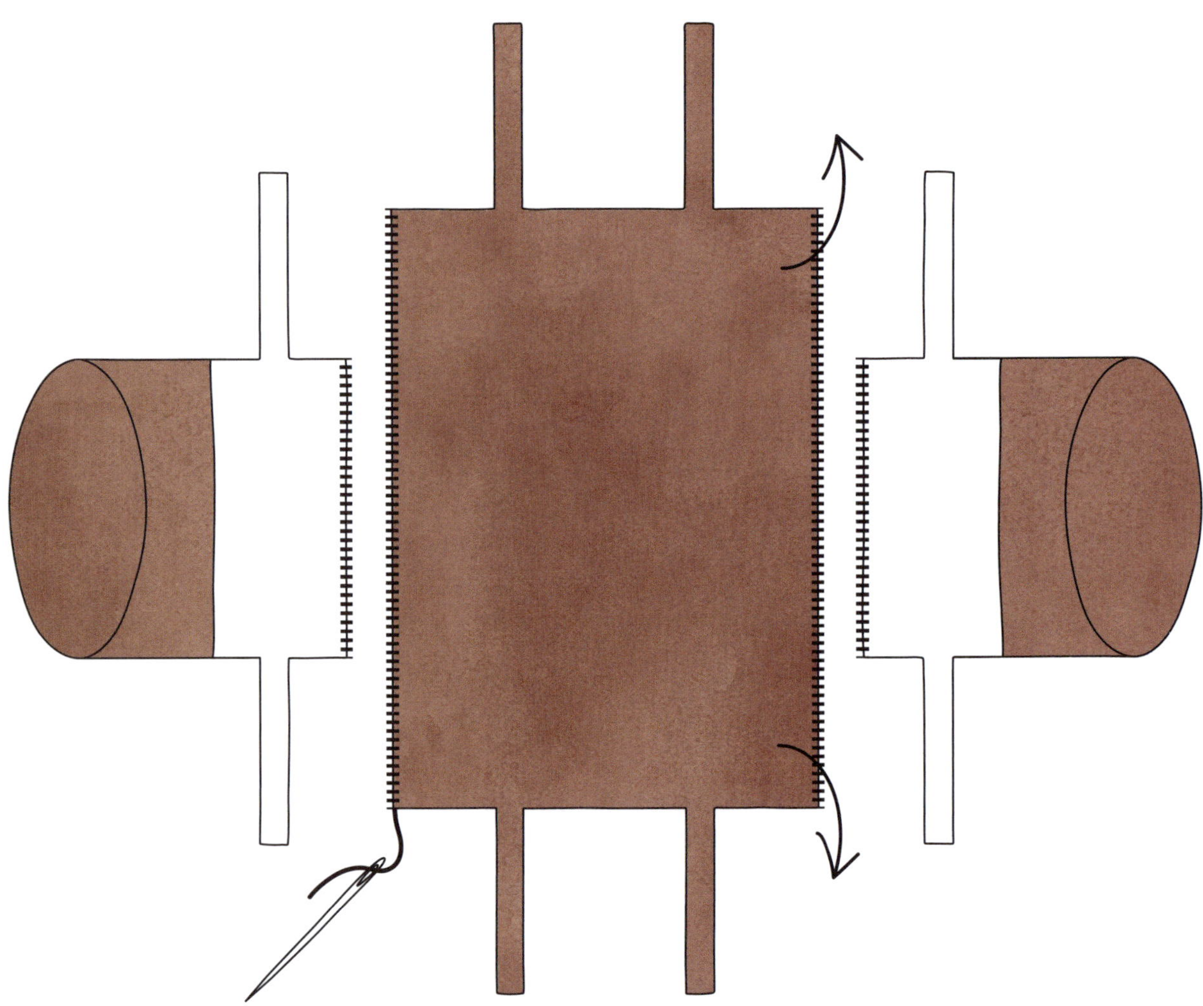

Inez blanket

The amazing granny square offers endless design opportunities. Here, a contrasting colour has sneaked its way in alongside the two main colours of this checked pattern, for a new take on the beloved, but sometimes a tad old-fashioned, granny blanket. There are patterns for two sizes.

CROCHET HOOK: 9 mm (US N/13)

YARN: chunky merino wool, super chunky (super bulky), 65 m/71 yd per 100 g/3½ oz ball

BIG BLANKET

YARN A (WHITE): 9 granny squares, 7 balls. Amount used: 675 g (24 oz)

YARN B (GREEN): 8 granny squares, 6 balls. Amount used: 600 g (21 oz)

YARN C (BROWN): 1 granny square, 1 ball. Amount used: 75 g/2¾ oz

OUTSIDE EDGE: 1 ball, approx. 55 g/2 oz

SMALL BLANKET

YARN A (WHITE): 4 granny squares, 3 balls. Amount used: 300 g/10½ oz

YARN B (GREEN): 4 granny squares, 3 balls. Amount used: 300 g/10½ oz

YARN C (BROWN): 1 granny square, 1 ball. Amount used: 75 g/2¾ oz

OUTSIDE EDGE: 1 ball. Amount used: approx. 40 g/1½ oz

EQUIPMENT: darning needle, scissors, sewing thread

STITCHES: chain stitch, slip stitch, double crochet, treble crochet, mattress stitch

TENSION (GAUGE): after row 1, the square should measure about 7 cm (2¾ in) square

MEASUREMENTS: big blanket: 72 x 144 cm (28¼ x 56¾ in), small blanket: 72 x 72 cm (28¼ x 28¼ in)

CONSTRUCTION: The blanket is made from 9 squares (small blanket) or 18 squares (big blanket). The squares are sewn together with mattress stitch and the blanket is finished off with a double crochet edge.

TIPS: Take your time. A square or two a day is enough.

Don’t worry too much about tension. A blanket doesn’t need to have exact measurements. As long as all your squares are the same size, your blanket will look great.

METHOD

Crochet in the round (in a square). The side facing you is the right side.
Ch 5 and join into a ring with a sl st into the first chain.

ROUND 1: ch 3 (counted as 1 tr here and throughout pattern), 2 tr into foundation chain ring, ch 2 (this is the first corner). Continue working in the round into the ring to the end of the round, *3 tr, ch 2* 3 times to make 4 groups of 3 sts (the first group is 3 ch and 2 tr), ending with a sl st into the top of the third chain. (12 tr, 4 x 2-ch sps)
The square should now measure about 7 x 7 cm (2¾ in) across. If the square is much bigger or smaller, now is a good time to adjust your tension.

ROUND 2: ch 3, *[3 tr, ch 2, 3 tr] in next 2-ch sp* 3 times, [3 tr, ch 2, 2 tr] in next 2-ch sp, end with a sl st into the top of the third chain. (24 tr, 4 x 2-ch sps)
The first three chain stitches make the third treble in the last group of trebles.

ROUND 3: ch 3, 2 tr in the same space between two groups of trebles, *[3 tr, ch 2, 3 tr] in next 2-ch sp, 3 tr in next space * 3 times, [3 tr, ch 2, 3 tr] in next 2-ch sp, end with a sl st into the top of the third chain. (36 tr, 4 x 2-ch sps)

ROUND 4: ch 3, 3 tr in next space, *[3 tr, ch 2, 3 tr] in next 2-ch sp, 3 tr in next 2 spaces* 3 times, [3 tr, ch 2, 3 tr] in next 2-ch sp, 2 tr in last space, end with a sl st into the top of the third chain. (48 tr, 4 x 2-ch sps)

ROUND 5: ch 3, 2 tr in the same space, 3 tr in next space, *[3 tr, ch 2, 3 tr] in next 2-ch sp, 3 tr in next 3 spaces* 3 times, [3 tr, ch 2, 3 tr] in next 2-ch sp, 3 tr in last space, end with a sl st into the top of the third chain. (60 tr, 4 x 2-ch sps)

ROUND 6: ch 3, 3 tr in next 2 spaces, *[3 tr, ch 2, 3 tr] in next 2-ch sp, 3 tr in next 4 spaces* 3 times, [3 tr, ch 2, 3 tr] in next 2-ch sp, 3 tr in next space, 2 tr in last space, end with a sl st into the top of the third chain, cut yarn. (72 tr, 4 x 2-ch sps)
Repeat until you have 9 squares the same size (for a small, square blanket) or 18 for the big one.

MAKING UP

Neaten up the squares by sewing in the loose ends. Make sure they are all roughly the same size.

1. Join the squares with mattress stitch, see page 27. The easiest way is to first sew 3 squares together and then join rows of 3 squares at a time. Sew loosely, about 10 cm (4 in) at a time and then pull stitches tight. Leave a decent amount of thread at the start and end of each row. I usually stitch these in at the end as it makes it easier to join the corners neatly.

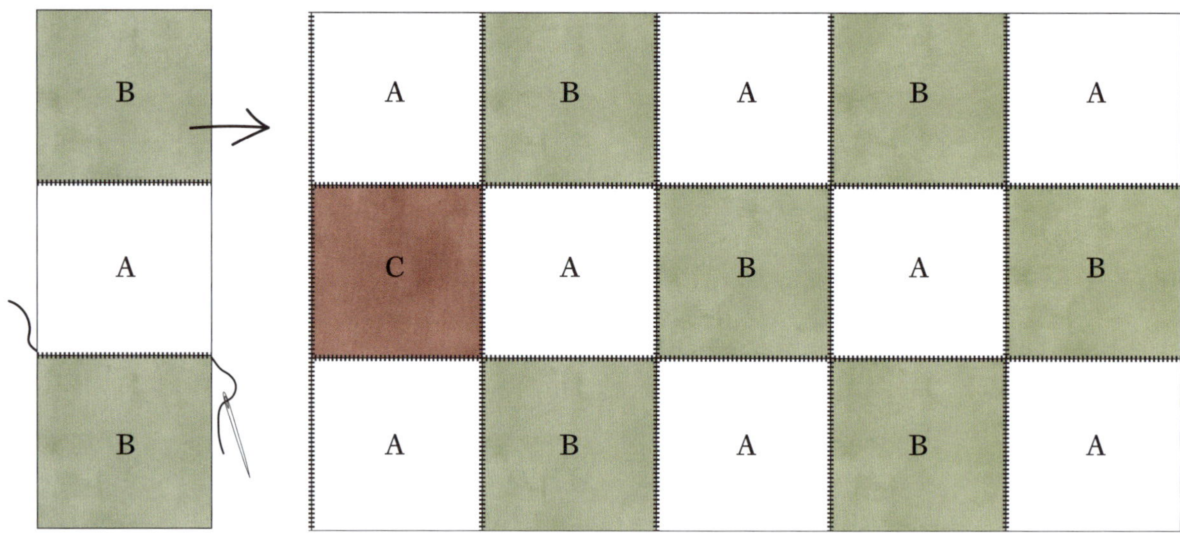

OUTSIDE EDGE

1. When you have sewn all the granny squares together, choose a colour for the outside edge of the blanket (approx. 55 g/2 oz). Attach the edge yarn to one of the corners. Work a row of double crochet around the outside edge of the blanket with an extra chain stitch at each corner. I chose to change the colour of my yarn to match the changing colours of the granny squares so that each square is edged with the same colour. But you could use one of the yarn colours to work the edge all the way round – or use a completely different colour to frame your blanket with a contrasting edge.
2. If you start at the short side of the blanket, the edge will be worked as follows: 60 (60) dc, ch 1 at corner, 60 (120) dc, ch 1 at corner, 60 (60) dc, ch 1 at corner, 60 (120) dc. Cut yarn and sew in the loose ends.

Knut cushion

Every blanket needs a matching cushion. I made eight bigger squares in three different colours for my granny cushion, and finished it off with an attractive double crochet edge.

CROCHET HOOK: 9 mm (US N/13)
YARN: chunky merino wool, super chunky (super bulky), 65 m/71 yd per 100 g/3½ oz ball (75 g/2¾ oz per granny square)
YARN A (WHITE): 4 granny squares, 3 balls. Amount used: 300 g//10½ oz
YARN B (GREEN): 2 granny squares, 2 balls. Amount used: 150 g/5¼ oz
YARN C (BROWN): 2 granny squares, 2 balls. Amount used: 150 g/5¼ oz + 25 g/1 oz for outer edge
EQUIPMENT: darning needle, scissors, sewing thread
STITCHES: chain stitch, slip stitch, double crochet, treble crochet
TENSION (GAUGE): After row 1, the square should measure about 7 cm square (2¾ in)
MEASUREMENTS: 50 x 50 cm (19¾ x 19¾ in)
CONSTRUCTION: The cushion is made from 8 squares, sewn together invisibly, and finished off with a row of double crochet around the edge.

You will need an inner cushion pad measuring 50 x 50 cm (19¾ x 19¾ in)

METHOD

Crochet in the round (in a square). The side facing you is the right side.

Ch 5 and join into a ring with a sl st into the first chain.

ROUND 1: ch 3 (counted as 1 tr here and throughout pattern), 2 tr into foundation chain ring, ch 2 (this is the first corner). Continue working in the round into the ring to the end of the round, *3 tr, ch 2* 3 times to make 4 groups of 3 trebles (the first group is 3 ch and 2 tr), ending with a sl st into the top of the third chain. (12 tr, 4 x 2-ch sps)

The square should now measure about 7 x 7 cm (2¾ in) across. If your square is much bigger or smaller, now is a good time to adjust your tension.

ROUND 2: ch 3, *[3 tr, ch 2, 3 tr] in next 2-ch sp* 3 times, [3 tr, ch 2, 2 tr] in next 2-ch sp, end with a sl st into the top of the third chain. (24 tr, 4 x 2-ch sps)

The first three chain stitches make the third treble in the last group of trebles.

ROUND 3: ch 3, 2 tr in the same space between two groups of trebles, *[3 tr, ch 2, 3 tr] in next 2-ch sp, 3 tr in next space* 3 times,

[3 tr, ch 2, 3 tr] in next 2-ch sp,end with a sl st into the top of the third chain. (36 tr, 4 x 2-ch sps)

ROUND 4: ch 3, 3 tr in next space, *[3 tr, ch 2, 3 tr] in next 2-ch sp, 3 tr in next 2 spaces* 3 times, [3 tr, ch 2, 3 tr] in next 2-ch sp, 2 tr in last space, end with a sl st into the top of the third chain. (48 tr, 4 x 2-ch sps)

ROUND 5: ch 3, 2 tr in the same space, 3 tr in next space, *[3 tr, ch 2, 3 tr] in next 2-ch sp, 3 tr in next 3 spaces* 3 times, [3 tr, ch 2, 3 tr] in next 2-ch sp, 3 tr in last space, end with a sl st into the top of the third chain. (60 tr, 4 x 2-ch sps)

ROUND 6: ch 3, 3 tr in next 2 spaces, *[3 tr, ch 2, 3 tr] in next 2-ch sp, 3 tr in next 4 spaces* 3 times, [3 tr, ch 2, 3 tr] in next 2-ch sp, 3 tr in next space, 2 tr in last space, end with a sl st into the top of the third chain. (72 tr, 4 x 2-ch sps)

Repeat until you have 8 squares the same size.

MAKING UP

Neaten up the squares by sewing in the loose ends (make sure they are all roughly the same size) before joining them together and you will avoid loose ends of yarn on the inside.

1. Join the squares with mattress stitch (see page 27) as shown below, making sure you have all the right sides facing the right way. Then repeat the same process to make the square for the back. The easiest way is to sew loosely, about 10 cm (4 in) at a time and then pull stitches tight. Leave a decent amount of thread at the start and end of each row. I usually stitch these in at the end as it makes it easier to join the corners neatly.

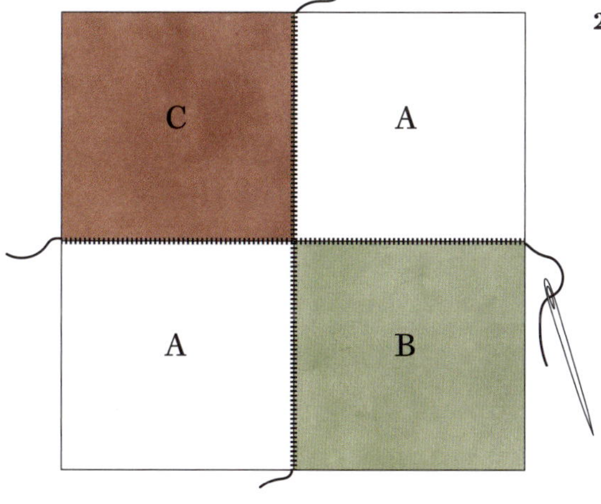

2. Place the front and back on top of each other, wrong sides together, with the right sides facing outwards. Choose a yarn for the outside edge of the cushion (about 25 g/1 oz) and join in at one of the corners. Work a row of double crochet around the outside edge of the cushion with an extra chain stitch at each corner. 40 dc, ch 1 in the corner, 40 dc, ch 1 in the corner, 40 dc, ch 1 in the corner, insert cushion pad and close the opening with 40 chain stitches. Sew in the remaining loose ends.

CAYUMAS
CAYUMAS

Cotton rug

A round rug, which will work equally well in the bathroom or the kitchen. This design gives you the freedom to explore changing colours and you can make the rug as big or as small as you like. A perfect project to use up spare yarn.

CROCHET HOOK: 12 mm (US P/16 or size to achieve tension)

YARN: 4 mm cotton yarn for macramé. Amount used: 825 g/29 oz, 165 m/180½ yd

EQUIPMENT: darning needle, scissors

STITCHES: chain stitch, slip stitch, double crochet, treble crochet

TENSION (GAUGE): 6.5 sts x 3.5 rows to 10 x 10 cm (4 x 4 in)

MEASUREMENTS: diameter 64 cm (25¼ in)

CONSTRUCTION: The rug is worked in one piece.

TIPS: Don't worry too much about tension. A rug doesn't need to have exact measurements. But bear in mind that you may need more yarn if you aren't working to the same tension as in the pattern.

Depending on your tension, you may need to remove or add one or two trebles per round to keep the rug flat. If the circle starts to curve inwards, you don't have enough increases per round and if it starts curving outwards, or becomes wavy, you have too many increases.

I changed colour randomly in this design, which often results in unique, abstract colour combinations. I'd like to encourage you to go for it – swap to a new colour whenever you feel like it. If you want complete rings in the same colour, change yarn when you start a new round. If you change yarn colour randomly, you'll get a beautiful abstract pattern instead. Or you can choose to make the rug in just one colour.

METHOD

Ch 5 and join into a ring with a sl st into the first chain.

ROUND 1: ch 2 (counted as 1 tr here and throughout pattern), 11 tr into foundation chain ring, end with a sl st into the top of the second chain. (12 tr)

ROUND 2: ch 2, *2 tr into the next space between 2 treble stitches* 11 times, 1 tr in last space, end with a sl st into the top of the second chain. (24 tr)

ROUND 3: ch 2, *2 tr in next space, 1 tr in next space* 11 times, 2 tr in last space, end with a sl st into the top of the second chain. (36 tr)

ROUND 4: ch 2, 1 tr into first space, 2 tr in next space, *1 tr in next 2 spaces, 2 tr in next space* 11 times, 1 tr in last space, end with a sl st into the top of the second chain. (50 tr)

ROUND 5: ch 2, *1 tr in next 3 spaces, 2 tr in next space* 12 times, end with a sl st into the top of the second chain. (61 tr)

ROUND 6: ch 2, *1 tr in next 4 spaces, 2 tr in next space* 12 times, end with a sl st into the top of the second chain. (73 tr)

ROUND 7: ch 2, *1 tr in next 5 spaces, 2 tr in next space* 11 times, 1 tr in next 5 spaces, end with a sl st into the top of the second chain. (83 tr)

ROUND 8: ch 2, *1 tr in next 6 spaces, 2 tr in next space* 11 times, 1 tr in next 5 spaces, end with a sl st into the top of the second chain. (94 tr)

ROUND 9: ch 2, *1 tr in next 7 spaces, 2 tr in next space* 11 times, 1 tr in next 5 spaces, end with a sl st into the top of the second chain. (105 tr)

ROUND 10: ch 2, *1 tr in next 8 spaces, 2 tr in next space* 11 times, 1 tr in next 5 spaces, end with a sl st into the top of the second chain. (116 tr)

If you want a bigger rug, that's easy. Follow the same pattern but increase the number of single treble stitches by one for each round, e.g.:

EXAMPLE ROUND 1: ch 2, *1 tr in next 9 spaces, 2 tr in next space* 11 times, 1 tr in next 5 spaces, end with a sl st into the top of the second chain.

EXAMPLE ROUND 2: ch 2, *1 tr in next 10 spaces, 2 tr in next space* 11 times, 1 tr in next 5 spaces, end with a sl st into the top of the second chain.
And so on.

ROUND 11: ch 2, 1 tr into every space all the way round, end with a sl st into the top of the second chain. (116 tr)

ROUND 12: Final round. ch 1 (not counted as a stitch), dc 116, end with a sl st into first dc.
Cut yarn. (116 dc)
Sew in the loose ends.

Washing & care instructions

Blocking, wetting your finished project and stretching the fibres to adjust the final shape of your crochet, is a common method for completing a project, but I prefer leaving the textile fibres to live their own lives and shape themselves over time with use rather than manipulating them by blocking.

I don't recommend washing crocheted garments. A wool garment is happiest if you avoid getting it wet. Hang it to air outdoors and the material will look after itself because it has self-cleaning properties. Stains are best dealt with using a damp sponge directly on the fabric. If you do want to wash your wool clothing, you should follow the instructions on the yarn you used to make it.

Cotton clothes tend to be quite hardwearing but the texture of chunky crochet does complicate things. Wash carefully in a bowl of cold water using a mild detergent. Dry your project flat to prevent it losing shape.

Jute is tough and hardwearing but not particularly easy to wash. It's best to get that damp sponge out again.

Your crocheted projects are happiest of all being worn. Otherwise, fold them neatly and put them on a shelf. If you put them on hangers, they can easily stretch and lose shape.

Measurements

MAIKEN T-SHIRT, PATTERN ON PAGE 85

SMALL = width approx. 42 cm (16½ in)
length approx. 42 cm (16½ in)
MEDIUM = width approx. 45 cm (17¾ in)
length approx. 45 cm (17¾ in)
LARGE = width approx. 48 cm (19 in)
length approx. 48 cm (19 in)
X-LARGE = width approx. 54 cm (21¼ in)
length approx. 54 cm (21¼ in)

MOORIT SLIPOVER, PATTERN ON PAGE 79

SMALL = width approx. 42 cm (16½ in)
length approx. 43 cm (17 in)
MEDIUM = width approx. 45 cm (17¾ in)
length approx. 44 cm (17¼ in)
LARGE = width approx. 49 cm (19¼ in)
length approx. 45 cm (17¾ in)
X-LARGE = width approx. 54 cm (21¼ in)
length approx. 46 cm (18 in)

FOREST CARDIGAN, PATTERN ON PAGE 99

SMALL = width approx. 65 cm (25½ in)
length approx. 54 cm (21¼ in)
MEDIUM = width approx. 71.5 cm (28 in)
length approx. 54 cm (21¼ in)
LARGE = width approx. 78 cm (30¾ in)
length approx. 54 cm (21¼ in)
X-LARGE = width approx. 84.5 cm (33¼ in)
length approx. 54 cm (21¼ in)

Yarn & substitute yarn

CHUNKY MERINO WOOL

WEIGHT: super chunky (super bulky)
YARDAGE: 65 m/71 yd per 100 g/3½ oz ball
TYPE: 100% merino wool in 12 colours
CARE INSTRUCTIONS: handwash only
AVAILABLE FROM: www.amandaljunggren.com
SUGGESTED SUBSTITUTE YARN: Viking Lovikka 100% highland merino wool, Järbo Lovikka 100% wool

BRITISH NATURAL WOOL

WEIGHT: super chunky (super bulky)
YARDAGE: 65 m/71 yd per 100 g/3½ oz ball
TYPE: 100% untreated wool in four shades
CARE INSTRUCTIONS: handwash only
AVAILABLE FROM: www.amandaljunggren.com
SUGGESTED SUBSTITUTE YARN: Viking Lovikka 100% highland merino wool, Järbo Lovikka 100% wool

COTTON RIBBON YARN

WEIGHT: super chunky (super bulky)
YARDAGE: 125 m/136 yd per 250g/8¾ oz ball
TYPE: 100% merino wool in 42 colours
CARE INSTRUCTIONS: machine wash at 30°C
AVAILABLE FROM: www.hobbii.com
SUGGESTED SUBSTITUTE YARN: Svarta Fåret ribbon 100% cotton

COTTON YARN FOR MACRAMÉ

THICKNESS: 4 mm
YARDAGE: 20 m/21¾ yd per 100 g/3½ oz
TYPE: 100% recycled cotton in 27 colours
CARE INSTRUCTIONS: handwash only
AVAILABLE FROM: you will often find cotton macramé yarn or cord in your local yarn or craft store

CREATIVE DECO JUTE TWINE

THICKNESS: 3 mm
YARDAGE: 300 m/328 yd per ball
TYPE: 100% natural, untreated jute
CARE INSTRUCTIONS: Do not wet
AVAILABLE FROM: www.creativedeco.co.uk
SUGGESTED SUBSTITUTE YARN: you will often find similar thicknesses of jute twine in your local hardware or DIY store

Index

Thank you

Thank you to Maiken. Without your patience, your good moods and your ability to sleep, there wouldn't have been a book at all.

Thank you to my pattern testers, Kay Kittilsen, Georgie Heatley, Ira Fotiadis, Ann-Cathrine Elmén, Lisen Trollbäck Eldh, Ellen Johansson and Anna Lindgren. Special thanks go to Cornelia Ivarsson who has crocheted practically every single project in the book. Thank you!

Thank you to Maria Yvell for your tireless efforts keeping the spotlight on crochet – whether it's a podcast or a festival – and even more thanks for creating a network of Swedish crocheters with whom you happily share your skills and experience.

Thank you to Johanna Lindahl/Mijo Crochet for your opinions and help with pattern writing.

Thank you to Tanja Bäcksvart/Tanja's Crochet for your detailed advice on pattern sizing.

Thank you to Mari Mattsson for the brilliant illustrations.

Thank you to Kerstin Neumuller for your opinions and advice.

Thank you to Laird Borrelli-Persson for being interested in my craft and for your wonderful interview for Vogue on the launch of my first collection.

Thank you to Joe for all your help creating the photographs for this book. For supporting my creative projects and being a devoted partner and father to Maiken.

Thank you to Mum and Dad, Matilda Alsteus and Sara at Knuten garn.

And most of all, thank you to you for taking the time to read and crochet projects from this book. If you have any thoughts or pictures of projects you would like to share, I'd love to hear from you.

www.amandaljunggren.com
Instagram: amanda_ljunggren

Quadrille, Penguin Random House UK,
One Embassy Gardens, 8 Viaduct Gardens,
London SW11 7BW

Quadrille Publishing Limited is part of the Penguin Random House group of companies whose addresses can be found at global.penguinrandomhouse.com

First published as Virka Stort

This English language edition published in 2026 by Quadrille, an imprint of Penguin Random House, in agreement with Bennet Agency

Published by Quadrille in 2026

www.penguin.co.uk

A CIP catalogue record for this book is available from the British Library

ISBN 978 1 8378 3644 4
10 9 8 7 6 5 4 3 2 1

Managing Director Sarah Lavelle
Editorial Director Harriet Butt
Assistant Editor Oreolu Grillo
Translator Kate Lambert
Photography Joseph Mercer-Holland
Illustration Mari Mattsson
Copy Editor Lindsay Kaubi
Cover Designer Katherine Beckwith
Designer Sebastian Wadsted,
Sarah Fisher
Head of Production Stephen Lang
Production Manager Sabeena Atchia

Colour reproduction by F1

Printed in China by C&C Offset Printing Co., Ltd.

The authorised representative in the EEA is Penguin Random House Ireland, Morrison Chambers, 32 Nassau Street, Dublin D02 YH68.

Penguin Random House is committed to a sustainable future for our business, our readers and our planet. This book is made from Forest Stewardship Council® certified paper.